THE TRUTH

THE LIE

and

THE BIBLE

THIRD EDITION

With much more information

BIBLE COMPANION
EVERY FAMILY THAT OWNS
THE HOLY BIBLE
SHOULD OWN THIS BOOK

BY SHADROCK

TO MY DAUGHTER
SOPHIA CARLOTTA
BORN OCTOBER 1965

FIRST EDITION 1990 ISBN 0-9694907-0-4
SECOND EDITION 1992 ISBN 0-9694907-2-0
THIRD EDITION 1995 ISBN 0-9694907-4-7

Cover Design by Author: SHADROCK
Printed in Canada
Fifth Ribb Publishing
P.O. Box 287, Station E.
Toronto, Ontario
M6H 4E2
Canada

PREFACE

This book is only made possible through the encouragement of my family in the House of Israel here in Toronto, Canada.

To Tony, Michael, the rest of the Family, the little Flock, and Laney whom I kept up late nights and called to duty early mornings, whose fingers must be bruised, or left imprinted on the keys of the computer. To all of you, please allow me to say in the most simple and sincere way - I love you all from the depths of my heart.

A special thanks to a great man of colour, whose name I bare, SHADROCK, my grandfather, who was my first earthly teacher. Whose voice I still hear telling me, "you are a Congo Pickney and a true born Israelite." Even though the earth has already consumed him, and his flesh is food for worms, his spirit lives within me and my memories. If my Grandfather was alive to-day, I know he would have been proud of me, but alas I would still attempt to speak on his favourite topic.

You see my grandfather never let a day pass without reminding me that I was a CONGO. I think his sister, my Great Aunt, AUNT CHARLOTTE was by far more demonstrative than my Grandfather. I remember one day she told Joyce (her adopted daughter) to ask me to fetch this huge bag of coal upstairs, for her to make her favourite dish of COUCOU, sometimes spelled coo-coo (an African dish popularly used by the older generation of Africans in some parts of the Caribbean, especially in Guyana and Barbados). She usually made the ochro (okra) stew or soup on a coal-pot (used as a stove, fuelled by burning coal). She was again telling Joyce to tell me to fetch the bag of coal, and Joyce was telling her that it was too heavy for me to lift. I can still hear my Aunt telling Joyce that I was a CONGO, and nothing was too heavy for me to lift. I can't remember how I did it, but that bag of coal was carried up those stairs by my small hands, and I never felt stronger in my entire life. I didn't as a young boy, knew how I felt back then, but as I grew older, I resurrected that pride, especially when I realized that I had lost them both.

I remembered the stories they used to tell me about Africa, the stories about the great kings of our homeland, the stories their Grandparents told them, for their Grandparents came out of slavery. Among all the stories they told me, not once did they fail to remind me that I was a CONGO. Not once did they forget to mention that we were all ISRAELITES.

I am older now, so I think I'll do the talking, hoping that they are in a position where they can hear me, and not on the side of torment.

A BRIEF HISTORY OF THE CONGO

FOR THE MEMORY OF MY GRANDFATHER
AND HIS SISTER

We will read in the pages to follow, how our forefathers travelled from the land Israel to North Africa, then to the Iberian Peninsula of Portugal, Spain and Italy, and to Western Africa to be made slaves to the New World.

Let's now deal with Portugal and how it affected the people of the Congo in particular - the people and place my grandfather felt a part of.

When these Israelites were thrown out officially from Portugal, by King John in 1484 they went to an island in Western Africa called San Thome, where others before them were. This island was discovered by the Portuguese earlier in the fifteenth century. It was operated by the Portuguese, the way the British operated Australia, as a huge jail. The reason for them being thrown in prison, was because of their refusal to accept Christianity.

They were known as the Black Portuguese. They eventually travelled to other parts of the area, places like CAMEROON, NIGERIA, SIERRA LEONE, SENEGAL, GAMBIA, GUINEA, GABON. Later on they occupied the lands around the CONGO RIVER, which included ANGOLA.

The Congo people were a great nation, ruled by great kings when Christianity came with the white Portuguese.

By this time Israelites were leaving Portugal in large numbers, and ruining the economy of that country. They fled from the wrath of Christianity and its white practitioners.

In 1496 King Manoel ordered all Israelites (he called Jews) out of Portugal by October of the next year.

6

He never expected such a shakeup of their economy, they merely wanted to drive fear into the minds of these Israelites, forcing them into becoming Christians. In early sixteenth century a decree was passed by the courts of Spain, forbidding them to leave, ordering them to become CHRISTIANS.

When the white Portuguese went to the CONGO, they saw a richness beyond what they were accustomed to. So in order to control this people with all of this vast wealth, they played with the people's emotions, just the way Christians do today.

In 1492, while Columbus was busy discovering America as they say, **NZINGA KUWU**, one of the greatest kings that ruled over this enriched Congo kingdom was conned into Christianity by these Portuguese.

How did this happen? First they told the chief ministers and captains, that they had found God, and how He had blessed them with a supreme Pontiff, and if he, King Kuwu wanted the same, he would have to give in to Christianity, which they called the universal religion. After consulting with his people, whom the Portuguese had already influenced, he gave in and became the first CONGO CHRISTIAN, and his name was changed from NZINGA KUWU to the Portuguese name of JOAO I. This is only one such story of how the Israelites lost their identity. Some Israelites had given it up for Christianity, while some gave it up for Islam, fearing persecution from both. Back to our story.

These white invaders brought with them all manner of sickness and disease upon the people of Africa. History also tells us of the sickness and disease they spread among the native Indians of North and South America, especially in Peru, where millions died of the sickness and disease of Europe.

Yes, just like Pa would say; "THERE IS SOMETHING OF A MIGHTY FORCE THAT'S KEEPING US FROM UNDERSTANDING."

I sometimes wondered how did Pa know so much, and he wasn't an educated man according to today's standard, but he sure was smarter than most Christian teachers I know, for I believe that Pa read THE PSALM OF ASAPH which speaks out against the Christians and the Muslims (Ishmaelites).

The plot against us had always been one or both, that is why one ended up selling us to the other. **Psalms 83:3-6**. "They have taken crafty counsel against thy people, and consulted against thy hidden ones.

They have said, Come, and let us cut them off from being a nation; that the name of Israel may be no more in remembrance.

For they have consulted together with one consent: they are confederate against thee:

The tabernacles of **Edom,** and the **Ishmaelites**; of Moab, and the Hagarenes."

They have not fully succeeded, for I would continue to be that voice shouting quietly in the wilderness of the Americas, keeping the promise of my Fathers.

LET THE NAME OF ISRAEL BE HEARD. LET IT BE SPOKEN BY LIPS THAT ARE WORTHY. LET THE REAL ISRAELITES STAND UP AND BE COUNTED.

To all my children, whom I have taught never to look for role models, but live towards the goal of being role-models themselves. Sophia, Penny, Perry, Angie and Stacy.

To Christians everywhere. Christianity is not the ultimate. Get out before it's too late. Remember God is not a Christian as you were taught, and if He is not, then you are alone.

Remember the words of Jesus in <u>Matthew 10:5-6</u> "These twelve Jesus sent forth, and commanded them, saying, Go not into the way of the Gentiles, and into any city of the Samaritans enter ye not: But go rather to the **lost sheep of the house of Israel.**"

This book is written to bring the truth and awareness to God's people, the Israelites, and all who wish to follow the one and only God: **The God of Abraham, the God of Isaac, and the God of Jacob. May my God that liveth in TRUTH** speak to you and guide you, as you turn the following pages.

THE TRUTH THE LIE AND THE BIBLE

THIRD EDITION

CONTENTS

INTRODUCTION

The word **truth** is what we hear about every time a Christian preacher takes the pulpit, facing his parishioners, or in the court of law, where a person is told to swear that he or she is going to tell the truth, the whole truth and nothing but the truth. These two areas are mostly influenced by the person in the spotlight at that given time, and in both cases, most of the time, the truth is not told, for that truth can be very damaging if known.

The pages that will follow in this book will attempt to set the record straight, and to define between the spoken truth, and the real truth. In as much as the man of the cloth shouts at the top of his voice about his truth, the quietness of the real truth reveals that **if something is not of the truth, then it is a lie,** and your strength as a person lies in the fact that loudness or emotion must not blind you from reality.

In this manner, you will be able to attain your sense of individuality. In this manner, you will be able to choose between the truth, and the lie. In this manner, you will be able to choose between the church, and your God. In this manner, you will be able to accept the responsibility of your own soul, and in this manner, you will be able to be yourself.

It is a fact that history is a record of events that indeed occurred, and can never change, but historians are merely human with emotions, that serve other humans, that inject philosophy and ideology in the minds of their subjects and because of these two factors history has been distorted to the core. In other words, history stands firm and in truth, while historians lie and lie again to support their lies.

This is not a book on history, for the writer does not see himself as a qualified specialist, however, where there are strong connections between the bible and the hidden truth, history will be mentioned to substantiate that truth. You will also notice in the pages to follow that Christianity is by far the loudest proclaimer of the truth and the biggest liar. Christianity has made its mistake by taking the holy bible as their official spiritual book of learning, and turned it around to be their official spiritual book of teaching. If one does not understand a subject, one cannot teach that subject, even though there is evidence that some Christians have come very close to the knowledge of the holy scriptures, but then it became so frightening that soon after World War II these panic stricken teachers and philosophers began to change words in the bible like black, and sentences and paragraphs that link black to the first civilization, so as to make that civilization white. Today there are numerous versions of the bible. Why?

They should have changed nothing, because there lies the evidence of their guilt. They should have created their own god, written their own book, and given it their own name, but instead they have chosen to hide the TRUTH, thus giving me the opportunity to expose these sophisticated liars.

Christianity has become the world's biggest lie and don't bother to look in the "Guinness Book of Records," because, along with being the super liar, their teachers are also very smart. To defeat Christianity will take the power of God Almighty, with His saints, His angels and His army. For the deceiver of the world is rich in wisdom, and while our God controls life and light, the deceiver controls death and darkness. Therefore, we must guard up our loins, put on new robes and welcome in the **Comforter who is the Spirit of Truth,** and fight on the side of the God of our Fathers, **the God of Abraham, the God of Isaac, and the God of Jacob,** when He comes to do battle, to conquer death, darkness and destruction. Together we will build that New Jerusalem. This is the time to join the army of truth, which is the army of GOD ALMIGHTY.

ABOUT THIS BOOK

This book is not about race or religion. It is not about philosophy or theology, yet, it is about all these things. This book is about the truth, not the kind of truth you hear about everyday on the lips of every two-bit preacher, trying to sell his philosophy and his understanding of the bible. This is the real truth, the way the bible was written for God's people, THE ISRAELITES.

This book is written to clarify and to set the record straight for all those who read the holy bible, regardless of your denomination. It is such a pity that I have to use the word denomination, but because of the LIES, it is now a real issue.

11

Did you ever stop to think that all Christians read the same bible, and yet they believe in different philosophies, criticize one another, blame each other, condemn each other and the poor parishioners who are caught in the cross fire, not knowing better, will always say - "my church does not believe in this, or does not believe in that" - **never what God wants, always the church.** Yet they go to church every Sunday, telling themselves and whoever would listen to them, that they are worshipping god. May I ask, which god?

Some of these facts will be very painful for the fanatical Christian, but all this book is asking you to do, is to prove it wrong and giving you the opportunity to choose between your God and your church. To some it will surely prove to be a very difficult task.

The bible is SPIRITUAL, HISTORICAL, PHYSICAL and PHILOSOPHICAL. So if you are a religious person, or a person that wants to know God, then the most important thing for you to do is to seek the truth first, with all of your heart and soul. All sixty six books deal with the truth, and you cannot believe in one part and not in another. This is the sign of the hypocritical behaviour of the Christian church, the teachers of false doctrine, not understanding anything that is of the truth. These teachers need to be aware of a very important fact. The apostles and others written about in the New Testament, read and taught from the Old Testament. The book of Daniel however predicted that this would happen. Daniel 7:25 states: "And he shall speak great words against the most High, and shall wear out the saints of the Most High, and think to change times and laws: and they shall be given into his hand until a time and times and the dividing of time."

After you have started to read this book, you might be enraged and feel like hating the writer. You might even want to call him names. Such reaction is acceptable, since it is only the old wine turning bitter. By the time you finish this book there should not be anymore old wine left in your vessel. I am sure that you will ask yourself a lot of questions and you will find the answers now that you have been made aware. Before, you might have had questions like: How could a white Moses have hidden in a black Pharaoh's house without being detected? This would mean that if Moses was white, then the Pharaoh had to be white, also the children of Israel had to be white.

The truth is, that during the time of Moses, the Egyptians were black, and this should change the course of your thinking. Whether the Pharaoh was Ramses II as written in conventional history, or Thutmose III(1486-1446 B.C.) (*See "The Word The Israelites and The Damned" page 55*). Moses a Hebrew was passing as an Egyptian. The children of Israel then had to be black. Then you may ask. Why do people try so hard to make all good things white and hate everyone that is black. Why do black people of the Americas, talk about God and Egypt with the same breath. Are we forgetting that it was the Egyptians who were the enemies of God and His people? Why are we so concerned about Africa as a place of salvation for us? Are we forgetting that Abraham refused to go back to Chaldea (Babylon), even stopping his servant from mentioning to his son about going back for his wife. He was very strong in his opposition. **Genesis 24:1-8**.

I believe that if one is not blessed with the Spirit of Understanding, that person should not be allowed to teach the children of slavery. A typical example: I recall one such liar and false prophet, telling his audience, and trying to convince them that they should all join the religion of Islam, because Sarah was really Abraham's sister, quoting **Genesis 20:12** refusing to tell the real truth as it is written in **Genesis 12:12-20** and to explain the generation of our father ABRAHAM in **Genesis 11:25-32**. We must put to shame these FALSE PROPHETS, regardless of who they are. Black people of the Americas are living in a spiritual hell, and looking for physical solutions in fancy speeches, that they will never find, unless they return to their God.

This book will prove how they changed the time and times, not only by writing their own bible, but by vigorously dressing up the lie with the clothing of truth.

Furthermore this book will prove that Jesus and His disciples did not drink wine at the Passover, that you cannot go to heaven, that the picture of Jesus is false. It will show that there is only one God. You will also learn about the worshipping of the Sun-god and Christianity, **the burden of the cross**, and who are the real children of Israel. But the most important thing is that this book will be telling you the truth, in a most simple, down-to-earth manner, starting from the Garden of Eden to the Revelation of John.

TRUTH THE SYMBOL OF GOD

Let's deal with reality, and reality comes from the word real, and if something is real it will belong to either one of the two extremes, hot or cold, dark or bright, good or evil, top or bottom, God or Lucifer, the truth or the lie. Then, let's see which side we're on because we are real, we live in a real world and we have real needs. We can either be good or be evil, we can either serve God or Lucifer. We can either be of the truth or believe the lie.

Now that this is made very clear, a believer in the true God, can no longer afford to compromise the truth. It either must be **the truth or the lie. God is the symbol of truth and Lucifer is the symbol of the lie.** It is very important for you to know your alliance and because some of you use the holy bible, the works of the people of God, their fate and mistakes, their power and their defeat, their richness and their poverty, the law and its consequences, the blessings and its glory. You can either believe in it or not, and if you believe in it, then, the power is in your hands to accept or reject the deceiver and liar. Given that the world we live in, is surrounded by scheming hypocrisy and lies, knowing the truth becomes our inner strength: for when you know the truth you feel secure in the alliance with God Almighty, and become the enemy of Lucifer, the liar. John 8:42-44 states: "Jesus said unto them, If God were your Father, ye would love me: for I proceeded forth and came from God; neither came I of myself, but he sent me. Why do ye not understand my speech? even because ye cannot hear my word. Ye are of your father the devil, and the lusts of your father ye will do. He was a murderer from the beginning, and abode not in the truth because **there is no truth in him**. When he speaketh a lie, he speaketh of his own: for he is a liar, and the father of it." The 45th verse says: **"And because I tell you the truth, ye believe me not."**

The bottom line is, you can't be of God and not seek the truth. For seeking is the only way to knowledge. If Moses stood on the flat ground, minding his own business, he would not have had that special relationship with God. He had to climb the mountain and face the fire, the element of God (the burning bush). The bible says in Matthew 7:7 "Ask, and it shall be

14

given you; seek, and ye shall find; knock, and it shall be opened unto you." Moses sought and he found God. He found truth. For John 8:32 says: "And ye shall know the truth, and the truth shall make you free."

Jeremiah 31:33 "But this shall be the covenant that I will make with the house of Israel; After those days, saith the Lord, I will put my law in their inward parts, and write it in their hearts; and will be their God, and they shall be my people." What do we learn from these scriptures?

With all the lies going around, mixed with confusion, you sometimes feel like throwing your hands up in the air, which is a very good sign of your individuality, rather than to stay and absorb all the false doctrines. You will be reading about the truth in later chapters. You question, and because you seek you will find. God is going to write His laws in your inner part. Then you will be able to clearly define the difference between the truth and the lie. For such a person will move heaven and earth if they could, to be on the side of truth.

Proverbs 23:23 says: "Buy the truth and sell it not; also wisdom, and instruction, and understanding." Knowing the difference between the philosophy of man, which in most cases is contrary to the truth and the true word of God is sometimes difficult because as I mentioned before, Lucifer is very powerful. Do not ever underestimate him, for he is very cunning and wise, and that is why strength in your belief must overpower all other weaknesses.

Colossians 2:8 states: "Beware lest any man spoil you through philosophy and vain deceit, after the tradition of men, after the rudiments of the world, and not after Christ." For if you allow this to happen, your destiny is written in Matthew 15:14 "Let them alone, they be blind leaders of the blind. And if the blind lead the blind, both shall fall into the ditch." How many people you know that will give all their loyalty to the church, even if they know that the church is not doing what God wants, but because of friendship or association with some unique clique, they will turn a blind eye, or pretend not to notice the wrong doings. The church takes upon itself to change God's law and to replace it with its own law, and in most cases breaks its own law, and tries to convince others that it is alright. The book of Matthew tells you about keeping the law and what it means to the Almighty God and

His prophets, for Jesus Himself said: Matthew 5:17-19 "Think not that I am come to destroy the law, or the prophets: I am not come to destroy, but to fulfill. For verily I say unto you, Till heaven and earth pass, one jot or one tittle shall in no wise pass from the law, till all be fulfilled. Whosoever therefore shall break one of the least commandments, and shall teach men so, he shall be called the least in the kingdom of heaven: but whosoever shall do and teach them, the same shall be called great in the kingdom of heaven."

Scriptures like this do not need interpretation, for a spade is a spade. When your teacher tries to interpret plain scriptures, it is a sign, that he or she is going to lie. Jesus is saying, that He didn't come all the way down here to change a thing. For He made the laws, and He appeared in the flesh, and what He chose to change He spoke of and nothing else.

In Luke 6:29 He said to turn the other cheek contrary to the law He had given by the hand of Moses, an eye for an eye. One must understand that this is not a contradiction but a difference in situation. When He gave Moses that law of an eye for an eye, the children of Israel were known for adopting the ways of the Egyptians. To commit one of the most gruesome crime, was the reason why this law was given. If an Israelite hurt a PREGNANT WOMAN, then it will be an eye for an eye for him, for one never know the gift of an unborn child. However, in the days of Jesus it was not only the unborn child, but he pleaded for compassion for all Israelites. " Thus it might well be, that rather than finding your brother and cradling him, you might treat him like the enemy So accept a blow from your brother rather than killing him.

Remember the story of David. II Samuel 18-19. In Matthew 5:21-22 "Ye have heard that it was said by them of old time, Thou shalt not kill; and whosoever shall kill shall be in danger of the judgment: But I say unto you, that whosoever is angry with his brother, without a cause shall be in danger of the judgment: and whosoever shall say to his brother, Raca, shall be in danger of the council: but whosoever shall say, Thou fool, shall be in danger of hell fire. Read to verse 24. Adultery was another law that He made stricter. The 28th verse states: "But I say unto you, That whosoever looketh at a woman to lust after her hath committed adultery with her already in his heart."

In other words, He was saying, don't use a woman as though she was a piece of meat. If you will have her then she is a part of your life. Bearing in mind that all these laws were not meant for the entire world, but given for the children of Israel by their Father, the God of Israel.

In all my findings there is not one piece of scripture where He mentions that He had changed the law, other than the blood at the altar. For He was now the sacrificial lamb, and every other law remains in tact. One must still keep the laws, the statutes and the commandments as requested by the prophets and being a lover of the truth is being a lover of God. <u>John 4:24</u> proclaims: **"God is a Spirit: and they that worship him must worship him in spirit and in truth."**

Again if the law is not written within you, the bible says that the lie will look like the truth, and the truth will look like the lie.

<u>II Thessalonians 2:9-13</u> "Even him, whose coming is after the working of Satan with all power and signs and lying wonders. And with all deceivableness of unrighteousness in them that perish; because they received not the love of the truth, that they might be saved. And for this cause God shall send them strong delusion, that they should believe a lie: That they all might be damned who believed not the truth, but had pleasure in unrighteousness. But we are bound to give thanks always to God for you, brethren beloved of the Lord, because God hath from the beginning chosen you to salvation through sanctification of the Spirit and belief of the truth:"

Do you think that this was written for the Christians of today? Well, if your answer is yes, then you are wrong. Simply because the bible is not a Christian book, it is a guide for the children of Israel, that is why today's Christians and Christian teachers are so mixed up and cannot distinguish between the truth and the lie. Every hero, every person of God written about in the holy bible is a child of Israel or follows the teachings of the children of Israel. The reason why the first chapter deals with how important the truth is to God and how important it is to know the truth, is because God is truth, and the devil is a liar. From now on, if you are a child of God, never make reference to anything pertaining to God Almighty and say that it is not important. The bible says "Seek and you shall find, knock and it shall be opened up to you." Aren't these words important?

17

If you do not know what is a spirit, how would you know when you see one? If you do not know what Jesus looked like when He walked the earth, how would you know Him in the Second Coming? Remember the bible tells us about all these false prophets coming before our Lord Jesus Christ returns to earth. All these demons of the earth will be praised by man, claiming that they are doing the works of God. How would you know dear reader? How would you know which is the right spirit?

I John 4:1 states: "Beloved, believe not every spirit, but try the spirits whether they are of God: because many false prophets are gone out into the world." and verse 6 reads: "We are of God: he that knoweth God heareth us; he that is not of God heareth not us. Hereby know we the Spirit of truth, and the spirit of error."

In Matthew 7:21-23 "Not everyone that saith unto me, Lord, Lord, shall enter into the kingdom of heaven; but he that doeth the will of my Father which is in heaven. **Many will say to me in that day, Lord, Lord, have we not prophesied in thy name? and in thy name have cast out devils? and in thy name done many wonderful works? And then will I profess unto them, I never knew you: depart from me, ye that work iniquity."**

When in doubt dear reader, question all statements made in the name of God because when Jesus left this earth, He said, when I go I will send the Comforter, and my dear friend the Comforter is the Spirit of Truth. The bible says in the book of John 15:26 "But when the Comforter is come, whom I will send unto you from the Father, even the Spirit of truth, which proceedeth from the Father, he shall testify of me:" And John 16:13 says: "Howbeit when he, the Spirit of truth, is come, he will guide you unto all truth: for he shall not speak of himself; but whatsoever he shall hear, that shall he speak: and he will shew you things to come."

This is to let you know the importance of the truth, and to let you know that the word of God is a mystery to most. It is only revealed to God's people and even the Gentiles that follow the word of the true God. In Colossians 1:26-27 "Even the mystery which hath been hid from ages and from generations, but now is made manifest to his saints." The 27th verse states: "To whom God would make known what is the riches of the glory of the mystery among the Gentiles; which is Christ in you, the hope of glory."

18

Christians say, just believe in the Lord Jesus Christ and thou shalt be saved. This is what the scriptures say, but what does it mean? Christians say all the commandments are rolled into one; "Love". Forget the commandments and just love. This is one of the most horrifying misconception of the true word of God.

First, let us deal with the believing in the Lord Jesus Christ and thou shalt be saved. In the 1984 American election, the Democrats believed in Mr. Gary Hart. He looked good and they believed in everything he said, and believed in everything he'd done. They were sure he was going to be the next Democratic President. Then according to the American people, Mr. Hart made a crucial mistake. He was seen in the company of another woman who was not his wife. In the 1988 election he was so far back of the pack for the Democratic nomination, that the number of Americans that voted for him was insignificant in comparison to the leaders of the pack. In other words he was no longer important. The people of America no longer believed in Gary Hart. This is a perfect example of what it means to believe in a person, or a philosophy. This is what it means to believe in the Lord Jesus Christ, "in totality." Believe in everything He says, believe in everything He has done, believe in everything He tells you to do. When you adhere to all these things, then that is the meaning of true belief, not just telling yourself and who ever listens to you that you believe in the Lord Jesus, and still doing the things He tells you not to do and ignoring the things He wants you to do. Believe means just what it says, believe does not mean half way, or for your own convenience.

You cannot believe in the Lord Jesus Christ and be saved in Christianity, once you are made aware that worshipping the Christian way is worshipping the way of the devil, worshipping the way of the Sun-god, worshipping the way of the queen of heaven, worshipping the way of Temmuz, Isis and Horus. In a later chapter, you will discover that Christianity is a compromise and there should never be any compromise in the worshipping of the true and living God.

Now we are dealing with the other Christian misconception. LOVE and the COMMANDMENTS. There is nowhere in the sixty six books where it says love is a total substitute for the commandments but this is what the Christians read. Galations 5:13-15 states: "For, brethren, ye have been called unto liberty;

19

only use not liberty for an occasion of the flesh, but by love serve one another. For all the law is fulfilled in one word, even in this; Thou shalt love thy neighbour as thyself. But if ye bite and devour one another, take heed that ye be not consumed one of another."

This is the scripture that all Christians use to manipulate the minds of the ignorant. Paul is pleading here with Israelites to love one another, because you can't say you love Christ and not love your brother sitting next to you. You can't go in the tabernacle to pray and not talk to your spiritual brother. You must have oneness of the Spirit before you can communicate with the Holy Spirit. That is what the bible says in Matthew 5:17-19. If you break the commandments you shall be called the least in the kingdom of heaven.

Even though the bible is so plain there is a different interpretation for every confusing denomination. It is time that people wake up, especially black people. The bible says that the people of God were not recognized only because they were good people. Some of them were terrible, as a matter of fact most of them were, but they were recognized by the simple fact, that they were of the truth.

I Kings 17:24 says: "And the woman said to Elijah, Now by this I know that thou art a man of God, and that the word of the Lord in thy mouth is truth." Even Jesus Himself told Pilate that the people of God will hear the truth. The bible says in John 18:37 "Pilate therefore said unto him, Art thou a King? and Jesus answered, Thou sayest that I am a king. To this end was I born, and for this cause, came I into the world, that I should bear witness unto the truth. Every one that is of the truth heareth my voice." How many times have you heard, "Oh! I am not interested in all those details, I just believe in God and I know that I am a nice person, I don't do any harm to anyone, I don't have any enemies, and I go to church every Sunday." If you were really a nice person in a truly religious sense you would seek the truth and not do the things the Christians do, like worshipping on Sundays, and believing in the lie as this book will illustrate as it unfolds.

The bible says in Revelation 22:18-19 "For I testify unto every man that heareth the words of the prophecy of this book, If any man shall add unto these things,   God shall add unto him the plagues that are written in this book: and if any man shall take away from the words of this book of the prophecy, God shall take away his part out of the book of life, and out of the holy city, and from the things which are written in this book."

Let's talk about plagues, and while we're on it, take a good look at the Blackman, and remember what God said that he would do to his children if they turn away from him. Do not look at others just take the beam out of your own eye, and take a good look in the mirror, and read what has been written in the book of Amos.

<u>Amos 3: 2</u> " **You only have I known of all the families of the earth: therefore I will punish you for all your iniquities".**

In other words, do not be too concerned about what the Christians or Muslims do, it is alright for them to do whatever they are doing. God will punish you, because you are his sheep (child), and a father will only punish his own. You should have been a leading example for others to follow, but instead you are following others and their false gods. "What a shame, now we have lost the power and the glory, and blaming the whiteman for everything, even when you kill each other you blame the whiteman. We have all become a generation of vipers, and we seek not that which is of God, but of Baal, we adore our church, and forget the truth about our God.

Dear reader, if you had an only child, and let us assume that child committed a terrible crime, was taken to the courts, and the judge depended on your statement of evidence to convict or repeal the charge laid against your only child that you love dearly - what would you do? You would tell a lie, but out of LOVE for your child, simply because the truth of knowing that your child is a criminal would hurt. Think about it. Can't you still love and break God's law? Can't you still love and lie? **Love is empty without truth. Moreover, love without truth is love without GOD.** You will still find a lot of good people, that are without God. So, therefore, being good is not necessarily being of God. Do not forget that Lucifer loves too, he loves his faithful servants. If you can love and lie, then you can love and be without God. Remember all spiritual experience is not always of God, for the devil is the greatest deceiver. **If there is no truth, then, there is no God: for truth is the symbol of God.**

21

THE FIRST FAMILY

Who was the first family? The first family was God Himself, and the angels. God resided supreme over all, and His second in command was Lucifer, later known as Satan, the Devil, etc. He was in control of the family government. His position was similar to that of a Deputy Prime Minister or a Vice President. He was in those days, "a Prince" second in command of the throne of God. We must know that the first family included Lucifer. This family had the knowledge of good and evil, because the Almighty God is a good teacher, and because of so much knowledge, the envy and the greed crept into the mentality of the very ambitious Lucifer. You see greed grows and undergoes the planning stages, then the implementation, and finally it evolves into the ugliness of hate, violence, corruption and the desire to overthrow.

All this happened in the first family-government. The lust for power, started with the first family, just the way it is today. The hidden lust came out, when the addition to the family was made.

There are some scriptures in this holy book of God, the bible, that sometimes can be very offensive to people. Today's woman is especially inclined to take offence, but a daughter of Israel should not. You daughters of the house of Israel should learn all about the mistakes that were made before your time, so that you do not make the same mistakes all over again. The scriptures do not say that only the sons of Israel will enjoy the fruits of their labour. Rather, **the whole house of Israel,** all the children, as long as they come to know God, and keep His laws, His statutes and His commandments they all shall be saved. So look at yesterday's woman with an open mind and correct yourself, pick yourself up when you fall and remember that the God of Israel is your GOD.

In the days of the first family God was the same way we knew Jesus to be in the flesh. He was flesh and bones and a natural person when He made Adam. He said, "let us make man in our own image and likeness." He was speaking to Lucifer and the others, even though He did it all by Himself.

Some people are confused about this whole statement of IMAGE AND LIKENESS, so I will try to explain it. First; IMAGE. The word image means, (1) "A representation of a person or thing, as a statue, picture, idol, etc.

22

(2) The picture or counterpart of an object produced by a lens, mirror, etc. (3) A natural resemblance, likeness, counterpart. (4) A mental picture, impression or idea. (5) The way in which a person or thing is popularly perceived or regarded:" This would mean that the image of a cow, would look like a cow in every way, therefore the image of a man would look like a man.

The meaning of the word, LIKENESS. (1) "The state or quality of being, a resemblance. (2) A copy, picture, or representation. (3) Similar in form." In other words, when God made the first man ADAM, He did not only make him in the image of Himself, but in His likeness. The cow on your mantelpiece is made in the IMAGE of the cattle in the field, but there is a particular one that bears the LIKENESS of colour, eyes, spots. etc. It is in this context that the first man was created, in the image and likeness of GOD, BLACK.

Let us return to the story that has confused others in their understanding of it. The plotting started by Lucifer and his faithfuls. You see Lucifer knew everything, except how to give the breath of life. "If I could only do that," he thought, "I would sit on the throne of the seventh Heaven," because this is God's domain. Now let us prove it with the scriptures.

First, let's prove that the flesh was before the spirit, and once that is proven, the point will be made that they in the first family were all flesh. I Corinthians 15:46 "Howbeit that was not first which is spiritual, but that which is natural; and afterwards that which is spiritual." That's why God said, "let us make man in our own image and likeness," because He was a man then. For Adam was not a spirit, he was flesh and bone, and God was the way we knew Jesus. He was a man, but a celestial man. All this changed on the first coup attempt to overthrow the government in power.

Lucifer lost that battle, but he is still in the war. Lucifer was not only powerful, he also had a lot of influence because of his beauty, and even today some people are able to exercise similar power and influence when others admire how handsome, or how pretty they are, and brush aside their real characteristics. The bible describes Lucifer in the book of Ezekiel 28:11-19.

"Moreover the word of the Lord came unto me saying, Son of Man take up a lamentation upon the King of Tyrus, and say unto him, thus saith the Lord God, Thou sealest up the sum, full of wisdom, and perfect in beauty. **Thou hast been in Eden, the garden of God;** every precious stone was thy covering. The sardius, topaz, and the diamond, the beryl, the onyx and the jasper, the sapphire, the emerald and the carbuncle and gold; the workmanship of thy tabrets and of thy pipes was prepared in thee in the day that thou wast created. Thou art the anointed cherub that covereth; and I have set thee so. Thou wast upon the holy mountain of God; thou hast walked up and down in the midst of the stones of fire. Thou was perfect in thy ways that thou wast created, till iniquity was found in thee. By the multitude of thy merchandise, they have filled the midst of thee with violence and thou hast sinned; therefore I will cast thee as profane out of the mountain of God; and I will destroy thee, O covering cherub from the midst of the stones of fire. Thine heart was lifted up because of thy beauty, thou hast corrupted thy wisdom by reason of thy brightness; I will cast thee to the ground. I will lay thee before kings that they may behold thee; Thou hast defiled thy sanctuaries by the multitude of thine iniquities, by the iniquity of the traffic; therefore will I bring forth a fire from the midst of thee, it shall devour thee, and I will bring thee to ashes upon the earth in the sight of all them that behold thee. All they that know thee among the people shall be astonished at thee; thou shalt be a terror and never shall thou be anymore."

These few verses do not need much explanation. It confirms that Lucifer was part of the first family, that he lived with God, and besides being powerful, he was also beautiful. You heard God's version of why Lucifer was cast down - because of the greed and the multitude of his iniquities. Even the devil's wisdom was corrupted, meaning that there is still wisdom in old Lucifer, but only to deceive and corrupt.

Now let's read what he (Lucifer) has to say in the book of Isaiah 14:12-14 "How art thou fallen from heaven, O Lucifer, son of the morning; how art thou cut down to the ground, which didst weaken the nations; For thou hast said in thine heart, I WILL ASCEND INTO HEAVEN, I WILL EXALT MY THRONE ABOVE THE STARS OF GOD; I WILL SIT ALSO UPON THE MOUNT OF THE CONGREGATION, IN THE SIDES OF THE NORTH: I WILL ASCEND ABOVE THE HEIGHTS OF THE CLOUDS; I WILL BE LIKE THE MOST HIGH."

This scripture proves that Lucifer, Satan, the Devil, whatever you choose to call him is still plotting his next move and one of his most ambitious plans is to sit upon the mount of the congregation - overlord - be in charge. Who would he lead? And what would he teach? It certainly wouldn't be the truth.

Let's go to another important part of the first family, Adam and Eve. How and where they lived, their culture, and their separation from the first family. We have learnt in Genesis that God made Adam from the dust of the earth, and blew the breath of life into him, and he became a living soul.

Now let's get into the details by examining Genesis 2:7 "And the Lord God formed man of the dust of the ground, and breathed into his nostrils the breath of life, and man became a living soul." This was the first terrestrial being, that is, the first earthly man who lived off the land. There was no sin committed during Adam's life alone in the garden. He was almost a satisfied man, but he had realized a difference: God and the other members of the family could do things that he (Adam) couldn't do. There was that invisible passageway between heaven and earth that was frequently used by the other members of the family and he could not use it. They would appear and disappear and he couldn't do that. He probably thought, "How could it be that they look like me...but are still different?" But the difference between the flesh and "the flesh" is that one is celestial, heavenly and has very little difference from the spirit. The other is earthly. A perfect example would be the way Jesus ascended up to heaven with His entire body.

So with all the company and all the control of the garden, Adam realized, just as God did, that he was lonely and needed companionship. Somebody like him, who could not disappear and appear. Besides, what good is a commander if there is no one to command. So according to the scriptures, God put him in a deep sleep, took a rib and made his companion, Eve. As mentioned in Genesis 2:21-23 "The Lord God caused a deep sleep to fall upon Adam, and he slept; and he took one of his ribs, and closed up the flesh instead thereof; And the rib, which the Lord God had taken from man, made he a woman, and brought her unto the man: And Adam said, This is now bone of my bones, and flesh of my flesh; She shall be called woman, because she was taken out of man;"

25

And so for the time being almost everybody was happy. Adam was happy, because now he had company. God was happy, because Adam was happy. But Lucifer was not happy because everyone else was happy, and there was still that little mystery that God did not reveal to him: "the Breath of Life." Lucifer thought that if he knew how to administer the breath of life, he would not have any need for the Almighty God. So began the envy and Lucifer's use of the spirit of jealousy. As we read before, evil was always there in the first family, but only in theory. It was against the principle of the teachings, to practise evil, even when the knowledge of evil existed. We will prove this later in this same chapter.

So Lucifer began to plan. He called his faithfuls together to work out strategies. Lucifer knew that he would never be able to be in total control if he was second in command, because God is forever, from the beginning to the end. God was not going to die so that he could take over. So the real ruler must have more knowledge in order to gain more power, but Almighty God is, "from everlasting to everlasting" and Lucifer refused to accept that.

As I said before, the knowledge of evil was always there. This is what the scriptures say in Genesis 3:21-22 "Unto Adam also and to his wife did the Lord God make coats of skins and clothed them; And the Lord God said, Behold, the man is become as one of us, to know **good and evil**, and now, lest he put forth his hand and take also of the tree of life and eat, and live forever." Now this scripture states: "Behold the man knows good and evil like us." Who is "**us**"? We know now according to the scriptures that although evil was there from the beginning, the actual practising of it started with Lucifer. Here is how it all began.

Like a tape recording, where the original is the best, because it is direct from the source. Every subsequent copy that comes from the original loses some quality, so it was with Adam and Eve. Adam was made by God, moulded with pride out of His own image and likeness. He was the first of the terrestrial beings. Now let us just sit back and imagine the feeling that the Almighty God must have had. Adam was the first, the original; then out of the original came Eve, the weaker sex. This being the case, Lucifer saw the opportunity to start the implementation of his plan by the courtship of Eve and the introduction of sex to her. Please

26

do not forget that he was a man like God and Adam. We have already discussed the difference between them. He then impregnated her with one or more daughters. We will prove this with the scriptures, because the Almighty God has given unto His people the wisdom to understand and to absorb the knowledge that is written in His word, the bible.

After she had her sexual experiences with the man, Lucifer, and bore their daughter or daughters, she then introduced sex to Adam, what she had learnt from Lucifer. According to the scriptures in Genesis 4:1 "Adam knew Eve his wife; and she conceived, and bare Cain, and said, **I have gotten a man from the Lord**."

Note here what she, Eve, is saying. Knowing that Adam was a special treasure to God and that God was now mad at Lucifer for what he had done, she believed that giving Adam a son was just like giving God Himself a son. Note again, she did not say a child; No! she said, "a man" from the Lord.

There is another piece of scripture to verify this fact that we have not been taught because there was no teacher to teach us. We have listened for generations to all the mixed up theories that have been taught in some universities and other institutions. But let us look at what is stated in Genesis 4:16-17: "And Cain went out from the presence of the Lord, and dwell in the Land of Nod, on the east of Eden; And Cain knew his wife and she conceived and bare Enoch, and he builded a city and called the name of the city, after the name of his son Enoch."

Remember that Adam was first, then God made his wife, Eve; then two sons came out of this union. Where then, after he had killed his brother Abel, would Cain find a wife? Aren't the scriptures telling you what happened between Lucifer, who was a man, and Eve? Imagine a woman baring her first child that opened her womb while still with her husband and it was not his? How bad she must have felt. So when she did give birth to her husband's child, she cried with joy and said, "I have now got a man from the Lord!" It means that she either did not have a son before, or none by Adam. One thing we should understand, is that man represents the seed while the woman represents the soil. This is just like when one plants a seed in the earth and expects to reap the fruit of that seed. Once you understand this you will

27

understand how Cain could take his sister. It was because they were not of the same father.

Now let's look at another aspect of the story of the triangle, the first of its kind. Now this forbidden tree was in the centre of the Garden and it contained strange knowledge, knowledge of good and evil. Later on we will deal with more facts that Lucifer was described as a tree even though we all know now that he was a man. What, may I ask, is in the centre of man, or, for that matter, woman too? How did they discover nakedness, and where do you think they were covering? They were covering up the centre of their bodies. That is where their loins were. We will prove later that Lucifer was the tree used as a parable and he used a serpent that tempted Eve.

Now, let's go over this very slowly. First, he was a man and the centre of the man's body resembles a serpent. This is parabolical. You may now draw your own conclusion. Lucifer was described as a tree, and the apple was in the midst, and it was the serpent who tempted Eve. Look at the biological resemblance of the serpent and the centre of a man's body. I will only deal with the scriptures now, again, I say that you must be wise enough to understand.

We now must prove that the apple, the serpent and the tree all had to do with Lucifer, Eve, and sex. Genesis 3:3-7 states: "But of the fruit of the tree which is in the midst of the garden, God hath said, Ye shall not eat of it, neither shall ye touch it, lest ye die..."

Let's try to analyse this verse. First, the fruit is in the midst of the Garden. We have already discussed this. We now move to the part where it is mentioned "Ye shall not eat of it." This eating can mean consume, or in a biological way where the vagina also functions as a mouth, because the next sentence says "neither shall ye touch it." To touch could mean to arouse, "lest ye die." The entire lifestyle of purity and serenity, the spiritual richness, the personal contact with God would all be lost and this was a form of death. The fourth verse reads, "And the serpent said unto the woman, ye shall not surely die," which means that they would be able to accept or reject God or Lucifer, death from godliness or life with the devil, for they did not die then physically. "For God doth know that in the day ye eat thereof, then your eyes shall be opened and ye shall be as gods, knowing good and evil," meaning that you could now make children, God did not have to take dust to make more men. "And when the woman saw that the tree was good for food, and it was pleasant to the eyes, and a **tree to be desired**, to make one wise, she took of the fruit thereof and did eat and gave also to her husband with her, and he did eat." There is a point to be noted here; SHE ate this fruit FIRST, THEN she took it to ADAM, so as we are discovering that this fruit has to do with sex, and she had it before she gave it to Adam. Who do you think she had it with? Bear in mind that Adam and Eve were ignorant about the function of the penis and vagina in terms of sex. To Eve, her vagina took in, so the word, "food", is used here. "It was pleasant to the eyes" meaning for the first time, the use of the penis in relation to her vagina was known. The next line states, "...and a tree to be desired." Now you and I know the meaning of the word desire, and therefore if when you put all this together, this new feeling, this harmonious satisfaction, that the three enjoyed, you will realize that Eve was having sex with both Lucifer and Adam. Adam's children were Cain and Abel, but Lucifer's children were not mentioned explicitly in the scriptures.

This was wisdom to Eve, because they were smart enough now to know that they were naked as stated in the 7th verse "And the eyes of them both were opened and they knew that they were naked and they sewed fig leaves together and made themselves aprons." Genesis 3:8 also confirms that they were all flesh and bones for they heard God walking even in their sinful state. "And they heard the voice of the Lord God walking in the Garden in the cool of the day; and Adam, and his wife hid themselves from the presence of the Lord God amongst the trees of the Garden." Point to note: **Man cannot hide from Spirit.**

And so this is how it all began with the first triangle. The identification of the serpent is found in Revelations 12:9 "And the great dragon was cast out, that old serpent, called the Devil, and Satan, which deceiveth the whole world, he was cast out into the earth and his angels were cast out with him." We know now that the natural was before the spiritual, because of this great disobedience by Adam and Eve influenced by Lucifer. God then became spirit form and separated Himself from man. Genesis 6:3 **"And the Lord said, My spirit shall not always strive with man, for that he also is flesh..."**

29

Soon after that Eve became the mother of all living, and her daughters were then known as DAUGHTERS OF MEN, while the males were known as SONS OF GOD, for it is now known that she begat daughters by the man Lucifer. The separation of the seed is mentioned in <u>Genesis 3:15</u> "And I will put enmity between thee and the woman, and between thy seed, and her seed. It shall bruise thy head and thou shalt bruise thy heal."

Let's read about her motherhood in <u>Genesis 3:20</u> "And Adam called his wife's name Eve, because she was the mother of all living." We know as it was said in <u>Genesis 3:22</u> God said "and take also of the tree of life, and eat, and live forever." Man did live forever, but through the process of insemination, the multiplication of the generation of terrestrial beings through sex, from the seed of man to the womb of woman; but Adam did not live forever, so this must be the process mentioned in the scriptures. It was also mentioned in <u>Genesis 1:28</u> "and God blessed them, and God said unto them, be fruitful and multiply, and replenish the earth, and subdue it, and have dominion over the fish of the sea and over the fowl of the air, and over every living thing that moveth upon the earth." This scripture is plainly saying to multiply means just that, to increase, to replenish the earth means to increase it all over again and again, and man can only do this through sex with a woman, not another man, or woman with woman, it must be man and woman.

There is something that we should all take very seriously. There was then no law against going to and fro, from man to man. In the eyes of Adam and Eve, she could have had sex with Adam when she felt like, or with Lucifer. There was no jealousy because of their ignorance, but then God made it very clear that it was wrong. In <u>Genesis 3:13</u> it is stated: "And the Lord God said unto the woman, what is this that thou hath done? And the woman said, The serpent beguiled me, and I did eat." This verse gives Eve's explanation for her actions. Here is where God told her it was wrong, and instructed her what to do. In <u>Genesis 3:16</u> "Unto the woman he said, I will greatly multiply thy sorrow, and thy conception, in sorrow thou shalt bring forth children: AND THY DESIRE SHALL BE TO THY HUSBAND: And he shall rule over thee" not forgetting that in <u>verse 6</u> she found Lucifer (the tree) desirable.

30

Let's deal with the tree. The tree is being used very often in the bible as a symbol of growth. It is also used as a symbol of the instrument of death and to describe Lucifer. First the scripture says in Psalms 1:3 "And he shall be like a tree planted by the rivers of water, that bringeth forth his fruit in his season; His leaf also shall not wither; and whatsoever he doeth shall prosper." This scripture clearly proves to us that parabolically, man is not very far in his likeness to the tree. There is another side of this spiritual growth that is like a tree and our body is made up like it. As it is written in Romans 12:4-5 "For as we have many members in one body, and all members have not the same office. So we being many are one body in Christ, and every one members one of another." Romans 11:16 states: "For if the first fruit be Holy, the lump is also Holy, and if the root be Holy, so are the branches."

We can read in Luke 6:43-44 "For a good tree bringeth not forth corrupt fruit; neither doth a corrupt tree bring forth good fruit. For every tree is known by his own fruit. For of thorns men do not gather figs, nor of bramble bush gather they grapes."

We have dealt with man's spiritual growth and how symbolic it is to the tree. Now we will deal with the tree as the man Lucifer, but before this we will deal with the description that he was a man. I would still like to quote another scripture describing him as such. Ezekiel 28:2 states: "Son of man say unto the prince of Tyrus: Thus saith the Lord God; Because thine heart is lifted up, and thou hast said, I am a God, I sit in the seat of God in the midst of the seas; yet thou art a MAN and not God, though thou set thine heart as the heart of God;"

So much for that. Now let's describe man as a tree, and imagine this man, sorry this tree giving the apple to a beautiful woman "Eve" and from this apple she realizes her nakedness, gets pregnant and takes the apple to Adam, and all the rest that goes with it.

Now let's see how the tree is a man. Read Ezekiel 31:7-10 "Thus was he fair in his greatness, in the length of his branches; for his root was by great waters. The cedars in the garden of God could not hide him, the fir trees were not like his boughs, and the chestnut trees were not like his branches, nor any tree in the Garden of God, was like unto him in his beauty. I have made him fair by the multitude of his branches, so that all the trees of Eden, that were in the Garden of God envied him; Therefore thus saith the Lord God, because thou hast lifted up thyself in height, and he hath shot up his top among the thick boughs, and his heart is lifted up in his height."

You can see how easy it was to influence Eve, with such power and beauty. It would have been hard for Eve to say no, because the Almighty God Himself was not as fair and as beautiful as Lucifer. It is stated in Isaiah 52:14 "As many were astonied at thee, his visage was so marred, more than any man, and his form more than the sons of men." As the scriptures reveal time and time again that Lucifer stood out in the crowd because of his beauty. So easy it was to seduce Eve, according to the scriptures, and so there were more children than Cain and Abel.

Let us continue the facts according to the scriptures which said that in those days, when Cain went off and married his half sister by the devil, the generation of his sister-wife was known as DAUGHTERS OF MEN and not of God, because Eve did not give birth to any daughter, fathered by Adam.

We read in Genesis 6:1-4 "And it came to pass when men began to multiply on the face of the earth, and daughters were born unto them, that **the sons of God saw the daughters of men** that they were fair, and they took them wives of all which they chose." Verse 4 states "There were giants in the earth in those days, and also after that when **the sons of God, came in unto the daughters of men,** and they bare children to them the same became mighty men which were of old, men of renown;" Have we not noticed here again the make-up of the daughters of men? This is what is said, "That they were fair." Wasn't this the same description of Lucifer, their father, fair and beautiful? We have also learnt that fair and beautiful is symbolic of evil, and not dark and ugly.

Again these are very lucid scriptures, and so began the generation from the first family, a mixture of good and evil - children of the first triangle. Do you still like the first family? Isn't the truth damaging? Do you think that a teacher of the truth will be loved? Think about all these facts, then think about all the things you have been taught before, bearing in mind the Comforter is the Spirit of Truth.

32

The bible says in II Timothy 3:7-8 "Ever learning, and never able to come to the knowledge of the truth. Now as Jannes and Jambres withstood Moses, so do these also resist the truth: men of corrupt minds, reprobate concerning the faith."

It is also said in Ephesians 4:14-15 "That we henceforth be no more children tossed to and fro and carried about with every wind of doctrine, by the sleight of men and cunning craftiness whereby they lie in wait to deceive. But speaking the truth in love may grow up into him in all things which is the head even Christ."

If you took a match and lit a candle, is it not physical? Your reason, however, might be spiritual. The physical action is always before the spiritual RE-ACTION. That is why it is so plain to see that the PHYSICAL WAS BEFORE THE SPIRITUAL.

Before I close this chapter of the first family, let me bring something else to mind which deals with the tree. Now you and I know that Jesus was crucified on a cross. It was written in the Roman law books that if any man breaks the laws of Rome and is found guilty, then the cross is one of the ways that he could be punished. So if the Jews prosecuted Jesus and found Him guilty, and He was sentenced to death on the cross why then does I Peter 2:24 state: "Who his own self bare our sins in his own body on the tree, that we being dead, to sins, should live unto righteousness; by whose stripes ye were healed." Why does it say here "on a tree"? Here the tree is the symbol of death. The tree is Lucifer, or Satan, and we are back again in the Garden of God, back again with the tree that represents death and destruction - the death and destruction that He will conquer in the Second Coming. Do not ever forget that even the cross was made with wood which comes from a tree. Just remember that the bible does not contradict itself. The tree is death. The tree is life. The tree is good. The tree is evil. Just like man, both good and evil, both strong and weak, both dumb and smart. But God reigns supreme - not the tree and thus begins the beginning of man and the search for the other family of God. **THE ISRAELITES.**

IN SEARCH
OF THE OTHER FAMILY

After the story of the first family ended, God continued to search for His family so that He would separate them from the rest of the world. Let's begin the story of our forefathers right from the very start.

According to the scriptures, the line had been drawn. Lucifer's new residence was earth. Such beauty and fairness all took a one way ticket to earth to create more beauty and fairness. Let's read about the separation between God and Lucifer in Ezekiel 31:16-17 "I made the nations to shake at the sound of his fall, when I cast him down to hell, with them that descend into the pit, and all the trees of Eden, the choice and best of Lebanon, all that drink water shall be comforted in the nether parts of the earth. They also went down into hell with him, unto them that he slain with the sword, and they that were his arm that dwelt under his shadow, in the midst of the heathen."

From then on, there were new happenings, new beginnings. The Creator was now set in establishing His family, but now the mingling of good and evil would always be there. The daughters of Lucifer inherited some of their father's ways and Cain was already a murderer who killed his brother, Abel, the one that God had loved. God had now decided to give Adam another son that he could love. Genesis 5:4 states: "And the days of Adam, after he had begotten SETH were eight hundred years:" So Seth was born and now God was ready to purge the earth and create His new family.

God had lost the physical bond with His first terrestrial son, Adam. Man could no longer mix with God, for God had now separated Himself from man by becoming a total spiritual being because man was now blemished (as you read in "The First Family.") Genesis 6:3. He therefore put spirit in man to add to his other two dimensions of body and soul, or soulful body, and with this spirit man would still be able to communicate with God, for Adam was without spirit because he was a living soul. In the generations to come God took on flesh again, but not in totality. God, as a spirit dwelt within Jesus and so the second creation of

34

a Son (flesh) was born, wherein the Spirit dwelt, which was Christ. I Corinthians 15:45 states: "And so it is written, the first man Adam was made a living soul, the last Adam was made a quickening spirit." Now God as a spirit was amidst a broken and separated kingdom, with the enemy on the other side. In this case, the domain of the enemy was on earth, the same earth He had created with the fullness of its riches. That same earth He had to cast the enemy upon. That enemy was Lucifer and his army. Now God was without His terrestrial family, and Lucifer, Son of the morning, was now the Prince of Darkness, Death, and Destruction. It is important that every government should have representation even in enemy country. Even though earth was not enemy country, because it was made by God, still the enemy resided upon it, and God therefore decided to create His own family to represent Him. So the search for this special people began.

We read in Genesis 4:16 "And Cain went out from the presence of the Lord, and dwell in the land of Nod, on the east of Eden." Now it has been known by biblical scholars that the land of Nod was not really a piece of ground situated in a definite place. Nod means to wander, so Cain wandered east of the Garden of Eden, which is known today as Iraq. At that time there was no division of land into continents, that's why the rivers are mentioned in the book of Genesis describing the location of the Garden of Eden. Genesis 2:10-14 says: "And a river went out of Eden, to water the Garden and from thence it was parted and became into four heads. The name of the first is Pison, that is it which compasseth the whole land of Havilah, where there is gold. And the gold of that land is good, there is Bdellium and the onyx stone. And the name of the second river is Gihon, the same is it, that compasseth the whole land of Ethiopia. And the name of the third river is Hiddekel that is it which goeth toward the east of Assyria and the fourth river is Euphrates."

The Hiddekel river is known today as the Tigris river, and the Gihon river is known as the Nile. The four heads coming out of these two rivers are The Great Zab, which is south of Nineveh; The Little Zab, which is south of The Great Zab; and also the Diyala River which flows into the Tigris.

35

In this area Cain started his family. The bible states that there were giants in the earth in those days and because everybody was black, the fairer skin stood out. For it was from this generation that the first organized society with a government on earth came. This area was called CUSH, later known as Ethiopia, where the people were described in the image of God: BLACK. Some historians might dispute by what name they were called at that time. The renowned black historian Mr. J.A. Rogers called them Grimaldis, or people of the Grimaldi race. Others might call them by different names, but neither black or white historians can ever dispute the fact that they were all BLACK.

You may read about the generation of Cain in the book of Genesis 5 and at the end of that chapter we come to the beginning of today's children. The 30th verse reads: "And Lamech lived after he begat Noah, five hundred ninety and five years and begat sons and daughters."

Now we must put our attention on Noah and his seed because it was from this seed that God chose His family. Noah's seed is written about in the 32nd verse: "And Noah was five hundred years old, and Noah begat Shem, Ham, and Japheth." and the scriptures state in Genesis 10:32 that the generation of Noah and his sons was the generation that filled the earth after the flood.

This is how the generation of Noah replenished the earth with different peoples, nations and kingdoms. Genesis10:6-7 mentions: "And the sons of Ham; Cush, and Mizraim, and Phut, and Canaan. And the sons of Cush: Seba, and Havilah, and Sabtah, and Raamah and Sabtecha, and the sons of Raamah; Sheba, and Dedan."

If you look carefully at the names of Ham's seed or offspring, you will find the generation of a great people emerging. For great cities bore their names. Cush were Ethiopians, Canaan the Canaanites; Seba and Sheba, comprised of almost the whole land of Africa ruled by very many great black leaders. The Queen of Sheba, Mekeda, being one of these leaders bore a son by Solomon named Menelik.

From the children of Shem came the children of Israel. Abraham was born in Ur of the Chaldea, which was Babylonia, or Babylon. This was south of the Euphrates, "The Garden of Eden", whose people were also black.

36

They lived in cities built by the generation of Ham, for it was the children of Ham that built the cities, and all the people could have been described then as "Cushite" which means black. The people could have been known as Ethiopians (which is the same as Kush or Cush). Their background, customs, appearance and culture were the same, until the incident at Babel which the bible spoke about. Here is where difficulty in communicating with each other began.

Each child, or tribe went its own way and formed its own culture, and thus begins the story of all nations. Out of this black family Shem, Ham and Japheth came all the nations that peopled the earth.

To get the biblical facts, read Genesis 10 & 11 to the birth of Abram, who God had made His promise with. You will also read that Japheth went to the Isles of the Gentiles and populated it. Hence, begat a generation of white skinned people, and Japheth's sons were known as Gentiles, which the bible describes as being wicked and violent. Genesis 10:2-5 "The sons of Japheth: Gomer and Magog and Madai and Javah and Tubal and Meshech and Tiras" and the fifth verse states: "By these were the Isle of the Gentiles, divided in their lands, everyone after his tongue, after their families in their nations."

So we will read that the people of God were identified in Abraham as Chaldean, similar in their culture as the Cushite, or Ethiopian. And the following chapters will identify the enemy of God. Revelation 20:8 says: "AND SHALL GO OUT TO DECEIVE THE NATIONS WHICH ARE IN THE FOUR QUARTERS OF THE EARTH, **GOG and MAGOG to gather them together to do battle. The number of whom is as the sand of the sea.**"

Ezekiel 38:1-3 states: "And the word of the Lord came unto me saying. Son of man, set thy face against Gog, and the land Magog, the chief prince of Meshech and Tubal." All these children were from Japheth, who went and populated the land of the Gentiles. They were known as Caucasians. The Isle of the Gentiles, is known today to be in the vicinity of Turkey (the Caucasian area). God also made this colour to become known as a curse when He placed leprosy on His own people and told them that they would be cursed and become white as snow.

The story of Miriam is a typical example. In Numbers 12:10 it says: "And the cloud departed from off the Tabernacle and, behold, Miriam became leprous, white as snow." In II Kings 5:27 is the story of another, Gehazi. "The leprosy therefore of Naaman shall cleave unto thee and unto thy seed FOREVER and he went out from his presence a leper as white as snow."

The enemy, from Lucifer, who was fair and beautiful, to the generation of Japheth who went north to the Isle of the Gentiles in the cold climate (where his seed was known as the enemy of God) was white. It is also noted that the curse that God put on His people was always turning them white. How then do Christians have A WHITE JESUS? and celebrate the feast of the Sun-God on the 25th of December, with a white Santa whose place is that of a god, ex: knowing when you're good or when you're bad, something that only God knows. It should be remembered too that the custom of his travelling is always from the North where he is always identified by the whiteness of his skin.

Japheth's generation is the enemy of God and the Caucasian mountains in Turkey are where the word Caucasian came from, to identify this people. Yet all Christian practices originated from the north, ex: Europe, when it is so clear that all of God's people were black. The very foundation of the children of Israel from Abraham to Jacob, David, Solomon, Job, Daniel, Jeremiah was black: ex: Abraham from Chaldea same as a Cushite. Solomon, Solomon 1:5 "I am black, but comely O ye daughters of Jerusalem..." As for the description of Jeremiah. Jeremiah 8:21 "For the hurt of the daughters of my people, am I hurt, I am black." It is stated in Job 30:30 "My skin is black upon me." To put it all together the people of God are described in Lamentations 4:8: "Their visage (face) is blacker than a coal." Believe it or not, no white person can become blacker than a coal, and even if by some miraculous shift of nature it happened, they cannot attain hair like wool, and Jesus had hair like wool, the symbol of the Blackman. Daniel 7:9 states: "I beheld till the thrones were cast down, and the Ancient of Days did sit, whose garments were white as snow and the hair of his head like PURE WOOL."

Please note that when the bible speaks of the race of people and not just the children of Israel, the word Ethiopian is used, for there were no people in those days called Africans. African was the name the Europeans called the Ethiopians.

38

Jeremiah 13:23 says: "Can the Ethiopian change his skin?" Psalm 68:31 says: "Princes shall come out of Egypt, Ethiopia shall soon stretch out her hands." and in Amos 9:7 "Are ye not as children of the Ethiopians unto me, Oh children of Israel?" All these scriptures identify God's people as the Ethiopian race, Africans. The reason why Miriam was cursed and turned white by God was because she was mad when Moses took an Ethiopian wife, not because they were of different skin colour, but because they worshipped different gods. It is also written in Revelation 1:14 "His head and His hairs were white like WOOL as white as snow." There are no scriptures stating Jesus or God being of the Caucasian race. Since we are now in the New Testament, we may also reflect on the person they called Paul. They mistook him for an Egyptian. Egyptians, especially in the days of Paul, were black. Acts 21: 38 then read Acts 13:1 "Now there were in the church that was at Antioch certain prophets and teachers as Barnabas and Simeon that was called Niger." Now Niger is a river and a country in Africa, and the people from this area were jet black. When the word Niger was used back then, it was merely to identify a people and their homeland. It was not an insult but soon after, somewhere between the fifteenth and sixteenth centuries, the Portuguese turned it into "negro" and later on as you well know, "negro" was turned into "nigger."

So to conclude the findings, and to end the search for the identification of God and His people, the answer will be "black." The children of Israel were all black, like their grandfathers before them, from Chaldea, to Egypt, and to Israel. I know I sound as though I am repeating myself, but I will never stop repeating this truth until every black person in the Americas understand who they really are, and at the same time not to be blinded by the word BLACK. We are all like AFRICANS in appearance, but we are different as a people. We were taken out of that race of people, just like our father Abraham was taken out of Babylon (Chaldea), and was preserved for God. Genesis 12:1-3 "Now the Lord had said unto Abram, **Get thee out of thy country, and from thy kindred, and from thy father's house,** unto a land that I will shew thee:
And I will make of thee a great nation, **and I will bless thee, and make thy name great; and thou shalt be a blessing:**

And I will bless them that bless thee, and curse him that curseth thee: and in thee shall all families of the earth be blessed."

First you would have noticed, that God told him to move out from among his family and from his country, then He will bless him. When you read the thirteenth chapter, you will discover that he moved away with Lot, but God had other plans for him, not his relatives, for GOD found a way to separate them.

There was a strife between the two sides that gave Abram a reason to call for a separation, and then God gave Abram the land. He had no intention to give it to Lot.

Genesis 13:8-9 "And Abram said unto Lot, let there be no strife, I pray thee, between me and thee, and between my herdmen and thy herdmen, for we be brethren.

Is not the whole land before thee? Separate thyself, I pray thee, from me. If thou wilt take the left hand, then I will go to the right; or if thou depart to the right hand, then I will go to the left."

After they had separated, this is what God told Abram. Verse 14-15 "And the Lord said unto Abram, after that Lot was separated from him, **Lift up now thine eyes, and look from the place where thou art northward, and southward, and eastward, and westward: For all the land which thou seest, to thee will I give it, and to thy seed forever."**

After this promise God explained who the seed of Abram would be, for it would not be the seed of Abram, but rather the seed of Abraham. First God identified Abram as the first HEBREW, knowing fully well that it would be through this line of Hebrews that the recognized seed would be.

Lets see where the line was drawn, and who was called Hebrew, and how. Genesis 14:13 "And there came one that had escaped, and told Abram the HEBREW."

GOD DID NOT TELL ABRAM TO TURN BACK AND LOOK FOR HIS ROOTS, but today every Jack and Mary is lost, looking for their so-called roots. We should all take a lesson from our father Abraham. Babylon went on to be the enemy of God, but Abraham remained God's servant. Abraham remained black like his fathers before him, but the children of Shem became an East Indian-looking people. We are Israelites, we were enslaved, and came to the Americas so that the scriptures might be fulfilled.

40

<u>Genesis 15:13</u>. We were made slaves just like our fathers, yet we do not understand. We are still blinded by the images of false gods, the same way our fathers were. Every false prophet comes to you with a gift of promise and really cannot deliver; but you really believe he can.

Christians tell you of a big fat universal love, that you were never a part of anyway, because nobody ever gave you a piece of that so-called love they talk about. Muslims tell you of a once powerful Egypt, and how once you were part of its glory. They tell you how Mohamed is the **shiloh** who came to save God's people. All these are lies. How can Mohamed be Shiloh, when he claims to be from the seed of Ishmael who was an Egyptian through his mother, and his offspring through his wife. For that matter Christians also believe that Jesus was Shiloh. All these are a display of complete ignorance. SHILOH was, and will be, an Israelite from any tribe of Israel except Judah.

SHILOH

Shiloh as a man was an Israelite, and will always be an Israelite, and can be no one else but an Israelite. As a piece of ground; it was attached to Israel for the benefit of the Israelites. All other statements are wrong, all other interpretations are incorrect. Take a slow walk with me through the pages of the scriptures, don't worry, I know where I'm going, for I am not blind, neither are you, if you throw away the white cane of the false prophets, who themselves carry their white canes of confusion.

When the word Shiloh was first used in the context of a person, it was used among the family of Israel. It was used by Israel himself to his sons, and it was to Judah in particular. <u>Genesis 49</u>. If you read from the the <u>eight verse to the twelveth</u> you will find that it was Judah's blessing, but right now we are concerned about the real meaning or definition of the word Shiloh, so lets read <u>verse 10</u>. "The SCEPTRE shall not depart from JUDAH, nor a lawgiver from between his feet, **UNTIL SHILOH COME; and unto him shall the gathering of the people be.**" We should always try to understand what we read. The word "PEOPLE" means Israelites.

First, the conversation is taking place among the sons of Israel, bearing in mind that Judah was given the sceptre to rule over all Israel. Now his father is predicting that he will rule, then when Shiloh comes, he, neither his seed (lawgiver between his feet) will rule, meaning, even though it was the Jews that were suppose to rule, there would come a time when another tribe would rule Israel, and not necessarily a child of Judah. Then history had provided us with the proof. It was a Levite that led the children out of Egypt (MOSES) a SHILOH.Read Exodus 2:1-10. The first king of Israel was a Benjamite (SAUL) another Shiloh, a non Jew (and unto him shall the gathering of the children be). Read Acts.13:21. So this means that even Jesus could not be a Shiloh, because he was a Jew.

Let's now try to dig deeper than your Christian or Muslim teachers. We are now going to examine the word as a piece of ground. Joshua 18:1 "**And the whole congregation of the CHILDREN OF ISRAEL assembled together at Shiloh,** and set up the tabernacle of the congregation there. And the land was subdued before them." This was where the Altar of God was built in the land of Canaan by the children of Israel, not the Ishmeelites or Muslims as you call them. It is highly impossible for Mohamed to be anything near Shiloh. Do not forget that it was the generation of Ishmael (Egyptians) that was the enemy of God and His people. We read again from verses 8-10 "And the men arose, and went away: and Joshua charged them that went to describe the land, saying, Go and walk through the land, and describe it, and come again to me, that I may here cast lots for you before the Lord in SHILOH.

And the men went and passed through the land, and described it by cities into seven parts in a book, and came again to Joshua to the host at SHILOH.

And Joshua cast lots for them in Shiloh before the Lord, and there Joshua divided the land unto the children of Israel according to their divisions."

As we read more and more we are discovering that Shiloh was never outside the jurisdiction of the children of Israel. You will also read the connection in Psalms 78. As a matter of fact, the only place where the Ishmeelites are connected to Shiloh, is where they killed God's people.

Read Jeremiah 41. You can read the entire chapter, but we will only quote from verses 5-7. "That there came certain from Shechem, from Shiloh, and from Samaria, even fourscore men, having their beards shaven, and their clothes rent, and having cut themselves, with offerings and incense in their hand, to bring them to the house of the Lord.

And Ishmael the son of Nethaniah went forth from Mizpah to meet them, weeping all along as he went: and it came to pass, as he met them, he said unto them, Come to Gedaliah the son of Ahikam.

And it was so, when they came into the midst of the city, that **Ishmael the son of Nethaniah SLEW THEM,** and cast them into the midst of the pit, he, and the men that were with him." This Ishmaelite lied, pretended to be on their side, then killed them. You may read the entire chapter for the complete story of deceit.

It is also said **in the Quran** that the message of God through his Prophets must come from the children of Israel, proof that not even Mohammed could have been a Shiloh.

S. XLV: 16. **"We did aforetime grant to THE CHILDREN OF ISRAEL the book, the power of command and PROPHETHOOD: We gave them for sustenance, things good and pure, and we favoured them above the nations."**

S. XX1X: 27. **"And we gave ABRAHAM ISAAC AND JACOB and ordained among his progeny PROPHETHOOD AND REVELATION and we granted him his reward in this life, and he was in the hereafter of the company of the righteous."**

S. 11:47 **"Children of Israel call to mind, the special favour which I bestowed upon you, and that I preferred you to all others for my message".**

We may now clean our mirror and take a good look at ourselves, all you children of slavery, for you are the children of ISRAEL. Again let me remind you that THIS IS NOT AN ISSUE OF COLOUR, BUT AN ISSUE OF POWER.

43

THE STORY OF ISRAEL
PART I

There are two very serious mistakes made by even renown scholars in law, religion, history, etc. and one wonders why. The first error is that most people think an Israelite is a person born in Israel. This is one lie that people should stay very far from. The other is that scholars call Israelites Jews. Some even make statements like, "These black Jews, some of the tribe of Simeon." You cannot be from the tribe of Simeon and be a Jew.

Let's now go back to the beginning of the children of Israel. All Jews were black. There should be no apology for this statement. As a matter of fact all Israelites were black. These Israelites were from the seed of their great grandfather Abraham, who was black himself and from the seed of Shem, who was also black. Remember it was the British convicts who settled in Australia and are now called Australians and black slaves from Africa who are now Americans and West Indians. They no longer used their old country's name. We read that Shinar was of Ham. Genesis 10:10-11 states: "And the beginning of his kingdom was Babel, and Erech, and Accad, and Calneh in the land of Shinar. Out of that land went forth Asshur who built Nineveh and the city Rehoboth and Calah." Iraq was also called Accad.

It says that in the beginning of his kingdom, Ham, Cush (Ethiopians) were in Babel, where they all went, all the sons of Noah. Before they went to Babel, the city of Babylon was already built by the seed of Ham. This land was also called Chaldea, the land of Abraham. It was at the Tower of Babel, where the difference of language and culture began. The scriptures plainly state who were the builders of the cities. It was the Ethiopians or Cushites, black people, who also built Sodom and Gomorrah. See Genesis 10:19-20: Egypt (Mizraim and Phut). See Genesis 10:6: Nineveh etc. East, West, North and South, even Lebanon (Sidon). See Genesis 10:15. History also tells us that the children of Shem, after the birth of Abram, peopled places like Mesopotamia to India, Pakistan, Afghanistan, while Abram remained in the midst of his brethren, the Ethiopians (Cush) and this was the foundation of **the children of Israel.**

44

They intermarried and cohabitated with one another until the time of Babel.There were no words like "Africa" and all of Noah's children then were like their father, **black.** They were known by the cities they built, by their father's name, or by the name "ETHIOPIANS" until Abram was known as the first Hebrew, and the father of the Hebrews. This was the background of the Israelites. Another nation that came out of Cush through Abraham was the Arabians, the children of Ishmael, who were Abram's seed, even though so many scholars still refer to Abraham as being a Jew. If Abram was a Jew, then so would be Ishmael, his first born, who was born of an Egyptian woman. Genesis 16:11 states: "And the angel of the Lord, said unto her, Behold thou art with child, and shalt bear a son, and shalt call his name Ishmael, because the Lord hath heard thy affliction." This was Abram's child and this child had grown to become the Father of Islam, who would dwell among his brethren. This means that a strong kinship developed between the rest of Abraham's seed, once they continued to worship the God that Ishmael's mother Hagar was introduced to. For it says in verse 12 "And he will be a wild man; His hand will be against every man. And every man's hand against him; and he shall dwell in the presence of all His brethren."

The children of Ishmael were blessed with their own blessing, and he still continues to dwell among his brethren. Many Israelites, as proven in history, became Muslims, some by choice, others through fear, especially at the time of slavery and in the height of the Muslim conquest of their vast world. We will learn, that the real Israelites fought alongside Muslims. We will also learn that in the days of the Egyptian glory, the children of Ishmael were so endowed with talent that they were equally powerful in creating another civilization. This mixture of Ethiopians and the children of Ishmael populated Egypt and made Egypt the world's most powerful nation - the mother of civilization. The Egyptians were the creators of astronomy, architecture, philosophy, magic and the basis for a true physical and spiritual society. Because of this power, the Egyptians started to see themselves as gods, and this was the cause of the crumbling of the Egyptian empire .In those days to conquer Egypt was to conquer the world. For the corner - stone of the world's civilization was in Egypt.

The children of Israel also had to be educated in Egypt, as we see in the story of Joseph (Genesis 42). The Greeks and the Romans were all educated directly or indirectly in Egypt. It was the dream of Alexander the Great to conquer Egypt, for only then would he be recognized as a true conqueror. We are not solely talking about Egypt but the very foundation of the children of Israel. Let us not forget also that Egypt would not have been so great, had it not been for an Israelite, JOSEPH, who made major political decisions at a crucial time in Egypt's history. Read Genesis chapters 41 to 48 for the story of Joseph.

Abraham begot a son, by his wife Sarah who was Hebrew. By this time God had made up His mind that indeed Abraham was going to be the earthly father of His children. He changed his name and made a covenant with him that would pass from him to his seed, and through their seed. Genesis 17:5-9 states: "Neither shall thy name anymore be called Abram, but thy name shall be Abraham, for a father of many nations have I made thee. And I will make thee exceeding fruitful, and I will make nations of thee, and kings shall come out of thee. And I will establish my covenant between me and thee, and thy seed after thee in their generations, for an everlasting covenant, to be a God unto thee, and to thy seed after thee."

Let's just try to evaluate all the statements above in verses 5-7. Please note that first He changed his name, and this was a sign that he was now in the family of the Almighty God. Meaning that he was now special in His sight, a rebirth, or a new life. After He had changed his name, He then made a covenant with him. He would be his God, and he (Abraham) would be His servant. Among all the people in this entire world, the Almighty God looked down and chose the seed of Abraham. These people meant something to God, for He had blessed them. I will continue to prove that this special people was chosen even before birth. Verses 8&9 reads: "And I will give unto thee, and to thy seed after thee, the land, wherein thou art a stranger, all the land of Canaan, for an everlasting possession and I will be their God, and God said unto Abraham; thou shalt keep my covenant therefore, thou and thy seed after thee, in their generations." Note, to get the richness of the spirit, the power, the glory, and prosperity in the land, you must KEEP THE COVENANT. It's the promise our Father Abraham made with God.

46

After the name- change and the covenant, and after God had prepared Abraham, the next stage would be to provide him with his seed that must be born after the rebirth of Abraham. The bible says in Genesis 21:2-3: "For Sarah conceived and bare Abraham a son in his old age, at the set time of which God had spoken to him. And Abraham called the name of his son that was born unto him whom Sarah bare to him, **Isaac**." Now this is only one son, and neither son or father were Israelites, or as the scholars state today, Jews. These two black men were Hebrews by custom and culture and Ethiopians by birth. This is the foundation that God had laid for His chosen. Then we go on to read, that Isaac grew up, took himself a wife of his own kindred, from his own generation known then as Chaldeans, or Hebrews. It is known that around the time of Abram's rebirth the word Hebrew was used. Abraham sent his servant to seek a wife for his son. He did not only say a wife. He was very specific. Genesis 24:37-38 states: "And my master made me swear, saying thou shalt not take a wife to my son of the daughters of the Canaanites, in whose land I dwell. But thou shalt go unto my father's house, and to my kindred, and take a wife unto my son." In other words Abraham was very careful because he knew that from this stock God would have His own children.

Let's see who was chosen to be Isaac's wife. Genesis 24:48 says: "And I bowed down my head and worshipped the Lord, and blessed the Lord God of my master Abraham, which had led me in the right way to take my master's brother's daughter unto his son." Her name was Rebekah as you can read in verse 45. This confirms that the background remained the same in the bloodline, colour, customs and heritage. Isaac and Rebekah were blessed from the covenant made between God and Abraham, which was passed on to Isaac, and then to Isaac's seed. Here is that story of Isaac's seed.

Before we move into one of the most important parts of this chapter let me also bring one more thing to mind, and here is food for thought. A confirmation of the people and the kinship of nations before the children of Israel were born. We have learnt that Rebekah was related to Abraham, a Chaldean, yet she was a Syrian. This is the prophecy of Abraham being a father of nations. This is also how the Ethiopians, being the first people,

47

populated the earth. They called themselves after the name of the city, Chaldeans, when it was Babylon they called themselves Babylonians, Egyptians, Syrians, according to their cities. Hence the relevance of the scripture Amos 9:7 where God combined these people together as one. The difference arose with the worshipping of false gods and strange customs because of the separation at Babel.

Let's still go on to prove that Rebekah being kin to Abraham was a Syrian, and continue on our story of Israel. Genesis 25:20: "And Isaac was forty years old when he took Rebekah to wife, the daughter of Bethuel, the Syrian of Padanaram, the sister to Laban the Syrian." Rebekah, according to the scriptures, was barren. Read verse 21. Then the Lord blessed her and she conceived, and a strange thing happened. She begot two nations, two different people. One was like their kind, and the other white (in biblical language, "red" which is the same as being leprous, or white). He was not the same as the rest of the family.

Genesis 25:23 says: "And the Lord said unto her, two nations are in thy womb, and two manner of people shall be separated from thy bowels, and the one people shall be stronger than the other people, and the elder shall serve the younger."

First, let us look at the prophecy, and the identification of the difference: "And the Lord said unto her; two nations are in thy womb, and two manner of people." Now Abraham's kindred were all black Ethiopians, and Ethiopians have woolly or kinky hair, but in the story we find that when Jacob, who was the younger brother went in to his father, pretending to be Esau the eldest, in order to obtain the blessings from his father, he had to wear the skin of a goat on his arm for his father to feel the straight hair. This identified that Esau was white with straight hair. Genesis 27:16 states: "And she put the skins of the kids of the goats upon his hands, and upon the smooth of his neck:" With this verse we identify the difference between them. As for the difference in manners, we would read where Esau strayed from the blood line in marriage to an outsider, a Hittite. Genesis 26:34-35 states: "And Esau was forty years old when he took to wife Judith, the daughter of Beeri, the Hittite and Bashemath, the daughter of Elon, the Hittite. Which were a grief of mind unto Isaac and to Rebekah." Here is where the generation of Esau was

48

becoming separate from that of his kinsmen.

HITTITES were white people in the history books, they were among the first people to occupy TURKEY. In the Bible however, they were known from the children of Canaan; Gen. 10:15 Heth the son of Canaan_(black-people with very light complexion.) In the old biblical times they worked for, and mixed with the Israelites. See story of BATHSHEBA an Israelite and URIAH the Hittite, in II Samuel.

The separation from the bowels meant from the time they were conceived they were different. "One people stronger than the other people, and the elder serving the younger." This can be found in II Kings when he rebelled against being ruled by the Jews. II Kings 8:20: "In his days Edom revolted from under the hand of Judah and made a king over themselves."

Let's read Genesis 36:1 to prove also that Esau is Edom. "Now these are the generations of Esau, who is EDOM." It was also prophesied by his father that the serving under his younger brother Jacob would come to an end. Genesis 27:40: "And by the sword shalt thou live, and shalt serve thy brother, and it shall come to pass, when thou shalt have the dominion, that thou shalt break his YOKE from off thy neck." Then God Himself had confirmed the difference by His statement about Esau in Malachi 1:3. "And I hated Esau..." Now that is the story of the brother that was not chosen. We know that he wasn't black and we know that he had straight hair.

Let's study the characteristics and happenings of Jacob the other brother. It was the custom of the people in those days that the first born would inherit their father's wealth. In this case Jacob was the younger son to Isaac, and the story about his blessing can be read in Genesis 27. To God, Jacob, was His first born, and just like He had done to Jacob's grandfather, He changed Jacob's name and made him His own son in order for him to inherit all that a father has to give to a son, especially a son that He loved. Genesis 35:10: **"And God said unto him, thy name is Jacob, thy name shall not be called anymore Jacob but Israel shall be thy name, and he called his name Israel."**

This is the Father of the chosen. A blackman from the seed of Isaac, from the seed of Abraham, who stayed in line with his parent's culture and custom and who worshipped the God of his fathers.

49

For his father Isaac called him and told him not to do the things that his brother had done. He told him that he must marry so the children could be of their kindred, and warned him about taking a Canaanite as a wife. Genesis 28:1-2. And Jacob was obedient and obeyed his earthly father. So he was made the first born of the Almighty Father. Exodus 4:22: "And thou shalt say unto Pharaoh, thus saith the Lord, Israel is my son, even my FIRST BORN." In Genesis 29 & 30 you will read about the children of Jacob who are the children of Israel. These are the sons of Israel from his first wife, Leah: REUBEN, SIMEON, LEVI, JUDAH, ISSACHAR, ZEBULUN. From Leah's handmaid, Zilpah: GAD, ASHER. From Rachel's handmaid, Bilhah: DAN, NAPHTALI. From his other wife, Rachel: JOSEPH and BENJAMIN. The seed or offspring of these 12 sons are known as the children of Israel, or the ISRAELITES. This is an example of how the individual tribes are known; either as the seed of - or in the case of Levi, a Levite. In the case of Dan, a Danite. In the case of Benjamin, a Benjamite, or in the case of Judah, a Jew etc. This means that all Jews are Israelites, but all Israelites are not Jews. This mistake is constantly made by scholars and historians. The bible said that all Israel, all twelve tribes were chosen by God, because He called them all His children, His son. Hosea 11:1 "When Israel was a child, then I loved him, and called my son out of Egypt." This was the end of God's search. He planned it from the day Eve became unfaithful and disobedient. The time He flooded the earth, and from the time He chose Noah, then Noah's seed; Abraham, then Isaac, and now His very own. Creator of the entire world, but Father only to ISRAEL.

After they had grown, and their father Jacob had blessed each and everyone according to their gift in Genesis 49, they had the world in the palm of their hands, their seed was overflowing with the blessings of their fathers. The Almighty God was now known as the God of Abraham, the God of Isaac, and the God of Jacob, and this name or recognition has never changed through all the generations, even in the time of Jesus the CHRIST.

THE STORY OF ISRAEL
PART II

Now the deceiver Lucifer, and his faithfuls; the Man from the North, the pagans, Gentiles, sons of demons, those that play gods deceiving the entire world and bringing upon a holy people a philosophy that they absorbed because of their hunger for the word. Christianity and its false gods has now dominated a people that have become so confused - left without a teacher, a people left without a home, left with leaders of false doctrines, leaders who are swallowed up in wine. These Israelites just like their fathers of old had forsaken their God. They had forsaken their God and ran after other gods, so God made them slaves to the Egyptians for four hundred and thirty years. People always ask the same question, every time it is proven that God's people were black. If they were indeed God's people, then why are they always at the bottom of the ladder and why are black people always despised and hated? The answer will always be the same. If your father that gave you everything took it back, and turned away from you then you would have nothing. For the Israelites received nothing on their own, but what was given to them by their Father, the Keeper of Covenant, but the children of Israel would not keep their part of the covenant then, and they still refuse to keep it now.

Ezekiel 39:23-24 "And the heathen shall know that the House of Israel, went into captivity for the iniquity, because they trespassed against me, therefore hid I my face from them, and gave them into the hand of their enemies. So fell they all by the sword. According to their uncleanliness, and according to their transgression, have I done unto them, and hid my face from them." The bible tells us time and time again how God sent a man from almost every tribe of Israel to warn these people, but they would not listen. Even after the first enslavement when He thought they had learnt their lesson and He gave them Moses, His servant, an Israelite from the tribe of Levi, a Levite, He still noticed their bent ways and stiff-necked attitudes.

First let's talk about Moses. He was not a Jew. Exodus 2:1-2 "And there went a man of the house of Levi, and took to wife a

daughter of Levi. And the woman conceived and bare a son..."
The 10th verse tells us the name of the child: "And the child grew, and she brought him unto Pharaoh's daughter, and he became her son, and she called his name Moses." Now we know that Moses was not a Jew and neither was Samson for he was from the tribe of Dan. Judges 13:24-25. "And the woman bare a son and called his name Samson, and the child grew and the Lord blessed him. And the Spirit of the Lord began to move him at times in the camp of Dan between Zorah and Eshtaol." These two examples are just to make you aware that all the biblical heroes were not Jews, but from other tribes of Israel.

Now you might want to ask, what connection or what relationship does the children of Israel have with the people of today, and who are their descendants. Christians see themselves different and distant from the Israelites. This is the way it should be, for Christianity has no part in the truth. An Israelite today should have no allies with any other strange philosophy, because they all took the idea of worship from the Israelite and changed it to suit themselves. Christianity being the worst since they replaced the God of Israel with their own philosophy.

Now let's go back to the connection or relationship to today, remembering and not ever forgetting the background of God's people. Jeremiah 49:15. "**For lo I will make thee small among the heathen, and despised among men.**"

The Blackman of the Americas must never forget this prediction, for when he forgets, the lie becomes the truth. Let's read Genesis 15:13 for the connections between...

THEN AND NOW

"And he said unto Abram, know of a surety, that thy seed shall be a stranger in a land, that is not theirs, and shall serve them and they shall afflict four hundred years." This scripture tells us of future things to come, for in 1562 Sir John Hawkins brought the first set of black slaves to the American colonies as captives. Four hundred years from then was the 1960's and if you are too young to know, ask your parents. This was the decade of a cleaning up and preparation. Read the last chapter "Christianity, the Lost Cause" for more details. The last enslavement really started around 1609 - 1611, the same time the King James version of the bible was published. Let's just take a look at the world from our front porch watching the closing in of the real four hundred years. Do not be confused about the time the children of Israel spent in Egypt. Read Exodus 12:40: "Now the sojourning of the children of Israel, who dwelt in Egypt was four hundred and thirty years. Also in Galations 3:17: "And this I say that the covenant that was confirmed before of God in Christ, the law which was FOUR HUNDRED AND THIRTY YEARS after."

For if these scriptures of four hundred years today were not so, then the following scripture will be irrelevant. God forbid. Deut.28:68: "And the Lord shall bring thee into Egypt AGAIN with SHIPS by the way whereof I spake unto thee. Thou shalt see it no more again, and there ye shall be sold unto your enemies for bond men and bond women and no man shall buy you."

Let's now break down this scripture and analyse it. "And the Lord shall bring thee into Egypt AGAIN" meaning that these people were in Egypt before, and since the United States and Britain were not known then, the name Egypt is used here as a symbol of oppression. The phrase "WITH SHIPS" clearly explains it, for in those days the camel and foot were the main modes of transportation. Besides, you didn't need ships to take you from Israel to Egypt or vice versa. "THOU SHALT SEE IT NO MORE." This means that the real children of Israel would not see that land any more. It goes on to say that the children would be sold in this strange land for bondsmen, meaning slaves. "And no man shall buy you." If you are sold, only common sense will tell you that the opposite of sold is bought. So why does it state no man shall buy you? This should have read, no man will want you, no man will love you, etc. because the same chapter gives the Israelites a prediction of the future. A first hand look is written in verse 43 & 44.

"The stranger that is within thee shall get up above thee very high, and thou shalt come down very low. He shall lend to thee, and thou shalt not lend to him, he shall be the head, and thou shalt be the tail." The stranger in this verse means philosophy and customs, for Christianity is unbeatable to most of today's Israelites (the descendants of slaves). Christianity is the ultimate and they feel that if you are not a Christian, then you are not of God. Yet they do not realize for one moment that not a single

53

person in the bible that they read was a Christian. That is how high the stranger is within them. This is the main reason why they, the strangers, can afford to lend, because they have to give, and the people of God cannot lend, because they are always in need. You watch great Israelites of the 1960s that came up, and were thrown down. Do you know why? This was a result of the hand of the Almighty God because the platform on which they stood was that of false gods, even though they were God's elect, yet they were deceived.

II Corinthians 11:14: "And no marvel for Satan himself is transformed into an angel of light." You must be able to evaluate the difference between the TRUTH and the LIE, for it is written in Matthew 24:24: "For there shall arise false Christs, and false prophets and shall shew great signs and wonders: insomuch that if it were possible, they shall deceive the very elect." This my dear reader is the power of Lucifer through the Christian church, or the teachings of Christianity. In the chapter dealing with "Christianity, the Lost Cause" we will prove how it is man-made, and in direct opposition to the word of God, but for now let's return to our subject.

We have learnt through the pages that all of God's people were black, and deep down inside I wish I did not have to repeat it so often, but I do not underestimate the LIE. You might now ask, how can I serve God if I'm not black? Fear not, for the truth is being told and even if you are polka-dot, your purpose should be to keep the laws, the statutes, and the commandments and to love God with all your body, soul, and spirit.

None of these chapters are dealing with race, they are all dealing with truth to the best of my knowledge. If the truth turns out that Jesus was black, or the Jews were black, or the House of Israel was black, then I say to you, SO WHAT?

The truth must hurt. When Jesus came upon this earth, He did not join the establishment, or social clubs called church. He did not go with the priests and pharisees, because the bible says that they were corrupted with false doctrines and philosophies. He went amongst ordinary people of his own culture. For He said in John 8:37-44 "I know that ye are Abraham's seed; but ye seek to kill me, because my word hath no place in you. I speak that which I have seen with my Father; and ye do that which ye have seen with your father.

54

They answered and said unto him, Abraham is our father. Jesus said unto them, If ye were Abraham's children ye would do the works of Abraham. But now ye seek to kill me, a man that hath told the TRUTH...Why do ye not understand my speech? Even because ye cannot hear my word. Ye are of your father the devil." Jesus was grieving here for His people. Like Paul said in Romans 9:6. "All Israel is not Israel, for they always turn away to other gods."

Do not forget that the Ethiopians are black, the Egyptians and Syrians are black, and in those days they were even more black. So why was Egypt the enemy of the children of Israel, and why did Miriam get mad when Moses married an Ethiopian woman?

Read Numbers 12:1: This was not because of race, for they were all black, but it was because they did not serve the same God. Amos 9:7: "Are ye not as children of the Ethiopians unto me, O children of Israel? saith the Lord. Have not I brought up Israel out of the land of Egypt?"

Let's go now to the New Testament in Matt.8:8-10: "The centurion answered and said, Lord I am not worthy that thou shouldest come under my roof, but speak the word only, and my servant shall be healed." This scripture is talking about a man who is not of Israel, he was a Roman, an enemy of Israel. Let's read what Jesus said to him in verse 10: "When Jesus heard it he marvelled and said to them that followed, verily I say unto you, I have not found so great a faith, no not in Israel." What about Cornelius? He was another Roman centurion, whom God told Peter that He had cleansed, for the Romans to an Israelite in those days were unclean, because of their false gods, their god of the sun, and their pagan ways. God said in Peter's dream that he was no longer dirty for he had cleansed him. (Acts 10:1-22). Here again it's not colour, but TRUTH. We all must worship the same God for there is no god given to His people, but the God of our Fathers, the God of Abraham, the God of Isaac, and the God of Jacob.Here's more proof that a learned man of Israel cannot be a racist. First, when I say Jews, know that they were black, for I hate to say black Jews. The other eleven tribes went all over Africa, the Iberian Peninsula of Portugal, Spain, Italy and Southern France. Also places like Cyprus, Turkey, India, where they were all called Jews. Like the famous Jewish Queen named Diah Cahena, who fought many great battles in Africa and soon after her defeat, her son became a Muslim. Black warriors conquered Sicily, and held it for forty years.

The Moroccan Kingdom consisted again of Israelites who later turned Muslims, when they conquered Spain in 711 AD. The armies were led by a fierce black Israelite called Tarif. He was from the tribe of Simeon. The island Tarifa, opposite Tangiers was named after him. Consequently Gebel al Tarik for which the Rock of Gibraltar was named took the whole Iberian Peninsula from 711 to 1485. Hence the blood of our fathers run in the Portuguese, Spanish, English, Italians, French, Turks etc. and according to the scriptures written in Ezekiel 47:22: "And it shall come to pass that he shall divide it by lot for an inheritance unto you, and to the strangers that sojourn among you which shall beget children among you, and they shall be unto you as born in the country, among the children of Israel, they shall have inheritance with you among the tribes of Israel."

Your neighbour means one with whom you can sit down together under a vine, or a fig tree, not the entire world. Read Zechariah 3:9-10. That's why we are told by our God to love our neighbour as ourselves. The bottom line is: All that worship the God of Abraham, the God of Isaac, and the God of Jacob, are family.

Remember, God did not punish His children for associating with other people, for most of them did. What God was concerned about, was the fact that they would be led away from Him, by these people and their false gods. In other words, let them get to know your God, never bend your knee to theirs. I Kings 11:1-2: "But King Solomon loved many strange women, together with the daughter of Pharaoh, women of the Moabites, Ammonites, Edomites, Zidonians, and Hittites. Of the nations concerning, which the Lord, said unto the children of Israel, ye shall not go into them, neither shall they come in unto you, for surely **they will turn away your heart after their gods.**" Before I get off the subject of the Israelites, let's exercise our knowledge in logic and history; facts and fiction; the truth and the lie.

FOOD FOR THOUGHT

Revelation 2:9: "I know thy works and tribulation and poverty, but thou art rich, and I know the blasphemy of them, which say they are Jews and are not, but are the synagogue of Satan." Now how can you be in poverty and still be rich? The richness comes from the things that money can't buy. Music, sports, manner of worship etc.

Revelation 3:9: "Behold I will make them of the synagogue of Satan, which say they are Jews, and are not, but do lie." Now black people have never called themselves Jews, for Israel is being referred to all over the bible as one with the sheep. For even Jesus said that He was a shepherd, and the symbol of the sheep is wool, and the hair of the black man is like wool. Matthew 25:33. "And he shall set the sheep on his right hand, but the goats on the left." Ezekiel 34:11: "For thus said the Lord God, Behold I, even I, will both search my sheep, and seek them out." Think also about the Lamb in Revelation, and the one sacrifice that was so Holy unto God, the SHEEP. Did you know Jesus was the Lamb of God?

Now let's give a fast look through history. Let's look at the four most powerful, popular and most influential presidents of the United States, the richest country in the world. The first president should have been the most popular, but he was not. Do you know why? Let me tell you why. He did nothing for the children of Israel. Instead Abraham Lincoln the sixth president freed God's children (slaves) and without knowing it had become a legend. Why isn't Thomas Jefferson the most popular president alongside George Washington? Do not forget that he was the author of the Declaration of Independence of the United States, which was one of the most important events in the history of the nation. I'll tell you why. He did nothing for the children of Israel. Instead John F. Kennedy the thirty fifth president, supported and approved the Civil Rights Bill, and he too became a legend. Can you remember what the only impeached president of the United States supported? Let all this be food for thought.

Think also upon this. Genesis 49:12: "His eyes shall be red with wine, and his teeth white with milk." In II Samuel 22:34. "He maketh my feet like hinds feet and setteth me upon my high places." This was our father David's gift. Now you tell me which people are strong enough to run as fast as a hind? And which people fit the description of red eyes and white teeth? Then you look at the picture of your Jesus on your wall and ask yourself. TRUE or FALSE, GOOD or EVIL, GOD or LUCIFER? Your answer will be your decision and your choice.

There is no hate taught in this chapter, only awareness. For it is written in Duet.23:7: "Thou shalt not abhor an Edomite, for he is thy brother, thou shalt not abhor an Egyptian because thou wast a stranger in his land." Try to analyze John 3:16: "For God so loved the world that he gave his only begotten son..." This is the only reason why He loved the world, because of His son. "That whosoever believeth in Him should not perish, but have everlasting life." DO CHRISTIANS believe in a BLACK GOD? For this is what the confusion today is all about.

THIS HOUSE WILL RISE UP AGAIN

We've been left out in the cold
Just like it was in the days of old
But this time we ought to know the truth
This time we ought to look for proof
For four hundred years is around the bend
This last four hundred
Is about to end

But sing it out loud my friend
Israel will rise up again
Egypt will never begin
To hold us under her wings
When the door is open
Let all of God's children come in

58

Moses wrote in Deuteronomy
After those days
Then we shall be free
But we must come back
Return to our God
Leave Christianity to Magog and Baal

No more white Jesus
He was a Jew and black
No more lies we exposed the plot
Of Christians who shout oh so loud
And Jews who are not

This house will rise up again
And all twelve tribes that is within
Egypt will never again
Hold us under her wings
Like this four hundred years of pain

Those who have eyes to see
Let them see
Those who have ears to hear
Let them hear
These dry bones shall live
And the
HOUSE OF ISRAEL
Will rise up again.

THE STOLEN COLOURS

According to history taken from the New World of Knowledge, p.225. "Before cloth flags started, Egypt, Israel and Syria used metal standards ascended on poles with animals or birds painted on them in specific colours. This was used to identify friend or foe in battle."

Hence, the beginning of colours which eventually represented countries. One of the first things taken from Africa by Europe, their symbol of identification. In the days when Egypt was militarily and economically strong, colours were of spiritual importance for their prosperity and might.

Men wore certain colours for certain events. They wore colours for birth, for death, colours for prosperity, colours for supremacy in battle, colours for love and colours identifying their spirituality. Most people do not understand the importance of colour. There are colours for babes in spirituality, colours for their Elders, their Priests and their Prophets. This is the way it has been through the generations. Today we look at the issue of colour, only in terms of skin-colour. If we do get pass this, we turn to the colours of today's Africa, which started sometime in the mid nineteenth century, when this new Ethiopia came into being under Menelik II. He ruled from 1844 - 1913 and built the new capital of Addis Ababa.

These colours of RED, YELLOW, GREEN AND BLACK used later on by Ghana, then by the rest of Africa, are not our true colours. This is part of the deception, and indeed a horrible mistake that is also contributing to our spiritual and economical decline. Being a spiritually receptive people, we must at all times be aware of the things we do. We are GOD'S chosen people and we should obey His words and not those of men. This is our major problem.

Now let's look at the children of Israel, who were the most powerful people, when they obeyed the God of our Father Israel, and when they worshipped no other god. Let's read how God gave our Fathers their colours, which we have inherited but have cast away for a poorer substitute, and made a mess of that inheritance. Our colours are RED, WHITE, BLUE AND PURPLE. The Romans were the first to steal the colour of supremacy, PURPLE. This became the colour of the emperors and then the colour of Rome. Next it was King James, who studied the works of our Fathers (the children of Israel). He wanted so much to learn about spiritual powers. Being a very smart king, an academic and scholar, who wanted mystical knowledge. James took reign somewhere in 1603, soon after in 1606 he ordered the flag of red, white and blue from the scriptures, OUR SCRIPTURES. Since Rome had the purple he must have thought, I'll take the rest, and the rest is history. This same king ordered the bible to be published in 1611.

In 1777, the United States did the same thing. You think again about these facts, they all speak for themselves, bearing in mind, it was a spiritual representative of the Christian faith, the Reverend Mr. Ezra Stiles, who influenced the congress to put 13 stars on the American flag of red, white and blue. These acts were not political, but rather very spiritual with in-debt reasons that took advantage on our spiritual ignorance. I tell you today, rather than going out and taking other colours that have no significant spiritual meaning for our prosperity - let's take our colours back.

Exodus 28:5 "And they shall take gold, and BLUE, and PURPLE, and SCARLET, and FINE LINEN." Take note that linen means plain white cloth. Scarlet means red. GOLD HERE IS NOT A COLOUR, but the mineral itself, as explained in Exodus 39:24-25. "And they made upon the hems of the robe, pomegranates of blue, and purple, and scarlet, and twined linen. And they made bells of PURE GOLD." Again it says in Exodus 28:6 "And they shall make the ephod of GOLD, of BLUE, and of PURPLE, of SCARLET, and of TWINED LINEN..."

Jesus wore a RED robe with a WHITE undershirt, and it was the custom of an Israelite to put BLUE at the seam in their undergarments. As you read in Numbers 15:38 "Speak unto the children of Israel, and bid them that make them fringes in the borders of their garments throughout their generations and that they put upon the fringe of the borders a RIBBAND OF BLUE." When they stripped Him, they put on Him the purple, that was then being used by the Roman leaders, so as to mock Him. Read John 19:1-2 "Then Pilate therefore took Jesus and scourged Him. And the soldiers platted a crown of thorns and put it on His head and they put on Him a PURPLE robe." You will also read

61

this in Mark 15:17-20. Verse 20. "And when they hath mocked Him they took off the PURPLE from Him and put His own clothes on Him." And what was His own robe? You'll find it in Matthew 27:27-28. "Then the soldiers of the governors took Jesus into the common hall, and gathered unto him the whole band of soldiers, and they stripped Him and put on Him a SCARLET ROBE."

Now common sense will tell you that He did not have on one simple robe only, JESUS WORE RED, WHITE, AND BLUE. It is red mixed with blue that gives you purple. What are you wearing? By choosing the wrong colours, you can be making a terrible mistake. The new Ethiopia, followed by Ghana and others needed their own identity. Weary of all the thieves of North America and Europe made another mistake, by laying the emphasis on political freedom, rather than spiritual freedom. Now Africa is left with the colours of red, green, yellow (you call gold) and black, and for the want of identity, gives you one hell of a choice. The choice to choose between colours that contributed to the downfall of the great empires of AFRICA, or to take back what is rightfully ours. As stated in Exodus 26:1. "Moreover thou shalt make the tabernacle with ten curtains of FINE TWINED LINEN, AND BLUE, AND PURPLE AND SCARLET..." Read Exodus 39:22. Read also Numbers 4:1-16. It tells you how important is the colour that you as a people don't use a lot of. BLUE.

The land of Israel today that got so mighty so fast, used this colour on their flag. The star of David is in blue. You have allowed the Edomites to progress through your ignorance. While you wear a map of Africa, and the colours of the damned around your neck, while others are wearing your colours, and progressing, you are sinking lower and lower in a state of hopelessness. The same way you make 13 your unlucky number, and shout every Sunday how you love Jesus. If He had 12 disciples, what was His number? What is 12 + 1 = ?

If there is any common sense or logic in what I'm trying to say, you will cease from using the colours of destruction to which you feel so attached. Remember every time you shout Africa, that God removed our father Abraham from among the Ethiopians in Chaldea, blessed him, made a covenant with him, then made

Chaldea (Babylon) his enemy and the enemy of the children of Israel, God also picked Moses out of Egypt, blessed him, and cursed the Egyptians. God picked His people out from the Canaanites then cursed the Canaanites. Do not ever forget that these people were all black, the Egyptians, the Ethiopians, the Canaanites. It was Africans (Muslims) who sold our Fathers into slavery to Christians. If we only learn to identify ourselves as the chosen of God first, and stop seeing the children of Israel as another people. If we could only put more emphasis on reality, and realize that we were picked out of Africa to be a special people unto God, our lives would be much better.

We are the chosen children of the circumcision. That is why we were made slaves like our fathers before us. We still walk in darkness the way they did. The reason why we are still in spiritual bondage is because we praise everybody else's god instead of our own. We kill each other rather than help each other and everybody else is right. Today you show such pride in the enemies of our Fathers, the Egyptians and the Ethiopians, worshipping their gods. Again forsaking the GOD of our Fathers.

Even if this is not true, look around you at the countries that use our colours of RED, WHITE, AND BLUE and see their progress, then look at the countries that use your adopted colours of red, green, yellow and black - then decide your spiritual fate.

Read what the pagan king's colours were in ESTHER 1:6."Where were **white, green** and **blue** hangings, fastened with cords of **fine linen** and **purple** to silver rings and pillars of marble: the beds were of gold and silver upon a pavement of **red** and **blue** and **white** and **black** marble." Ahasuerus was a ruler of old Ethiopia, and all this new Ethiopia did was drop the most spiritual colours of Purple and Blue, and replaced them with the poorest of substitute:"Yellow" Then read what the colours of Mordecai were? Esther 8:15. Bearing in mind that Mordecai was an Israelite from the tribe of Judah, A JEW. Esther 8:9.

Think about all these facts and remember to take those colours of red, green, yellow and black from your possessions and replace them with the colours that are approved by OUR FATHER, GOD HIMSELF. Exodus 39:43 "And Moses did look upon all the work, and behold, they had done it as the Lord had commanded, even so had they done it; and Moses blessed them:" They wore the colours of red, white, blue and purple.

63

THE CROSS

This is the most devastating symbol of worship. This instrument wrecked the once powerful inner-being of the Blackman. The worshipping of, or with, the cross by the Blackman generates total depression, false anxiety of all his dimensions, for he is very receptive spiritually, and because of this, it is very important to always be spiritually aware. Not the kind of awareness that will turn you into a fanatic, but rather that of sound knowledge about this subject. To some people, a spirit is a spirit. This belief is extremely dangerous to a person, and harmful to the community in which they dwell.

I, therefore, make no apology when I tell you that the cross is evil. If you want to worship God, never use a cross, for to use the cross is to worship the dead. Let's take a good look at this cross. The cross was invented by pagans (Roman rulers), in order to kill, punish, and destroy God's most important creation, MAN. How can you then say it is holy? God never said it was holy. Jesus never said it was holy, and the bible never said it was holy. Then let's see who said that.

It was Constantine, a pagan. In 312 A.D. when he marched on Rome to do battle with Maxentius, he claimed that he had a vision from heaven to use the cross. Throughout biblical history, God has never given a sign to a pagan. Constantine used his authority and lied to gain favour among God's people, who were then underground in the Roman Empire. These Israelites, the same ones that were called Christians in Antioch. Acts 11:26. He supported their ways to gain their confidence. He then later changed everything about the worshipping of the real God, to the worshipping of the sun god and Isis, and all the pagan gods like the easter goddess of spring. So by the time this so-called religion was exported, it was no longer of God, but of man. In another chapter we will deal exclusively with the birth of Christianity.

Let's go back to the cross. First it started out as a killer, the instrument of death (sin). Then man changed it, and called it holy. Tell me something? If Jesus was alive today and they hanged Him, would you call the rope holy for killing our Lord? It is the same way that they call the day they killed Him, GOOD (Good Friday). The day they claimed that he was born, is celebrated with

64

wreaths (a sign of death), instead of bouquets of flowers. There is also an X, which means omission, confirming his absence from this celebration (XMAS).

Let's see what the bible has to say about the cross, bearing in mind that the cross is inseparable from death. It kills! It caused the destruction of God's people. It is unclean. What does the bible say about the dead? Numbers 19:13-14. Verse 14 "This is the law, when a man dieth in a tent all that come into the tent, and all that is in the tent shall be UNCLEAN seven days." In the books of Moses it says very clearly how unclean are the dead, and everyone or everything that comes in contact with the dead are unclean. Mark 12:26-27: "And as touching the dead, that they rise, have ye not read in the book of Moses, how in the bush, God spake unto him, saying, I am the God of Abraham, and the God of Isaac, and the God of Jacob, He is not the God of the dead, but the God of the living; ye therefore do greatly err." Take a good look around you at the so-called spiritual person who uses the symbol of the cross and look at his life. Not just any person but a spiritual, black person. Other people have their gods, and their gods are not for the Blackman. **"The god of the Gentiles you should not serve, for you are chosen above all people." says the Lord.**

Then let's look at a black community, or nation. The more spirit they generate, the more they descend into poverty. How about the spiritual capitals of the world of voodoo, like Haiti and Brazil? Their worshipping is empty without a cross, and so are the open devil worshippers. Again the cross is being used by KKK to kill black people. The cross was used in Africa by these very pagans, to indoctrinate our fathers. Now let's read the scriptures the Christians use to brainwash black people, and let's see what kind of cross is written there, whether it's the cross of Christ (His death), or any cross made by man today. I Corinthians 1:17 "For Christ sent me not to baptise, but to preach the gospel, not with the wisdom of words, lest the CROSS OF CHRIST should be made none effect." This scripture simply means that the death of Christ will be made none effect, meaning He would have died in vain on the cross. Before you get two pieces of wood and nail them together, remember to be very, very careful of the type of spirits you'll be encouraging.

I John 4:1: "Beloved believe not every spirit, but try the spirit, whether they are of God." This instrument of death should be treated for what it is. Let's look at another scripture that is responsible for this dreadful mistake. Luke 14:27: "And whosoever doth not bear his CROSS and come after me, cannot be my disciple." All Jesus is saying is that if you cannot bear the pressure, don't follow me. In other words, count the cost. People are going to laugh at you, mock you they might even kill you. Note too, that Jesus was alive and well not dead, if you are therefore worshipping the cross because He died on it, then what cross was He talking about here?

If you can't swim don't go in the water. Let's see what the 26th verse says: "If any man come to me, and hate not his father, and mother, and wife, and children, and brethren, and sisters, yea and his own life also, he cannot be my disciple." Would you now go out hating everybody, and say you saw it in the bible? Then your spiritual blindness is beyond repair. For this very same God said to love your parents and your brethren.

Exodus 20:12. "**Honour thy father and thy mother** that thy days may be long upon the land which the Lord thy God giveth thee." The 28th verse sums it all up: "For which of you intended to build a tower, sitteth not down first, and COUNTETH THE COST..." There is no need to be blinded anymore. Let's all stop worshipping sin, for to kill is a SIN, and we know what the cross is a symbol of. Romans 6:6 states: "Knowing this that our old man is crucified with him, that the body of sin might be destroyed and henceforth, WE SHOULD NOT SERVE SIN."

Let's use another scripture to discover the truth and to unearth the lie. Galations 6:12: "As many as desire to make a fair shew in the flesh, they constrain you to be circumcised, only lest they should suffer persecution for the CROSS OF CHRIST." Also in the 14th verse, "But God forbid that I should glory save in the CROSS OF OUR LORD JESUS CHRIST." All these scriptures are telling you about the **Cross of Christ.** The one cross that killed Him, that old rugged cross, that is now rotten and no more. Do not give glory to wood and stone. For the cross was not made for Jesus and Jesus alone, just like the bullet was not made for Dr. Martin Luther King and Malcolm X. The cross was made for breakers of the Roman law, thieves, bandits, revolutionaries, killers, people who were sick in the spirit. The home for the cross is the cemetery.

66

That's why, it is the custom of Christians to take the dead to their altar. Could there be light at an altar of the DEAD? The same altar where they pray. How can an unclean dead body be in the same place where you worship the true and living God, when He said that He is not a God of the dead? That's why He also said, let the dead bury the dead. For if your spirit is of the dead, then you are qualified to be with the dead. Luke 20:37-38.

Give the Romans back their cross. The cross is made of WOOD and the Romans put a false picture of a white Jesus made of STONE and the scriptures say in Deut. 28:64: "And the Lord shall scatter thee among all people from the one end of the earth, even unto the other and there thou shalt serve other gods which neither thou, nor thy fathers have known even WOOD AND STONE." The confirmation of all this can be seen in some black churches, where they even have the symbol of the sun on their altar. I tell you my people, take heed.

Ephesians 4:14: "That we henceforth be no more children, tossed to and fro, and carried about, with every wind of doctrine by the sleight of men, and cunning craftiness, whereby they lie in wait to deceive."

These statements in the bible are so misinterpreted that sometimes it is hard to tell the truth from the lie. That's why the structure of Christianity must be taken down and examined piece by piece. Did you know that the first altar in Rome, where the Romans claimed to have been converted to Christianity, was built on DEAD BODIES? They buried bodies under their altar, using the same shrines of their goddesses for Christian services along with their cross.

The bottom line: Christianity uses the cross as a sign of worshipping the dead, and as my people waddle in the wilderness of ignorance the situation is becoming worse. The symbol of the cross is the symbol of the tree.

I Peter 2:24: "Who his own self bare our sins in his own body on the tree, that we being dead to sins, should live unto righteousness by whose stripes ye were healed." This will help you to understand that a true person of God **celebrates the resurrection, not the death, nor any symbol, nor any instrument, nor tool that caused death. For of such it will be unclean.**

67

The group labelled as devil-worshippers or satanic by Christians should know that the effect of whatever they do will remain intact with the cross standing, the way it does in Christian churches.

These satanics will discover that they do not have to turn the cross upside down. Similarly, voodoo worshippers who do not turn their cross upside down.

The Christian body is just another group of devil worshippers. They worship the dead in a more sophisticated way. To deal with the cross is to deal with the dead, and to deal with the dead is to deal with the unclean spirit who lives and dwell among the dead. Mark 5: 2 "And when he was come out of the ship immediately there met him **out of the tombs** a man with an **unclean spirit.**"

Colossians 2:14. **"Blotting out the handwriting of ordinances, that was against us, which was contrary to us,and took it out of the way, nailing it to the cross"**

Suddenly now we are all clinging to this same cross that now contains everything that is contrary to us, and working against us.

There is much more proof of the relationship between the Christian church, the dead and Paganism.

Ask your Christian preacher next Sunday when you attend your little country church, why is the church surrounded by tombs and graves? Why do I have to jump over, or walk over dead bodies to worship God?

What do you think the Christians do? Do you think they really worship the true and living God? NO! leave the cross in the burial place, do not bring this unclean instrument at the Altar where you pray. Remember this instrument of death, along with the drinking of wine at your altar, has caused the Blackman's downfall.

The Christian church is just more organized, most influential and larger, but nevertheless the smoke from their incense-pot goes in the same direction, towards darkness.

This message is particularly for the Blackman, and all those who are spiritually aware. Be sure you entertain messengers of God, rather than demons that follow after the cross.

TO WORSHIP THE CROSS, IS TO WORSHIP THE SPIRIT OF THE DEAD.

TO WORSHIP THE DEAD IS A SIN, A DAMNATION UNTO GOD.

THE REAL SABBATH

Let's look at how many commandments the Christian church or Christianity has broken.

ONE - Thou shalt have no other gods before me. Christianity has replaced Him with the man from the north. Fair and beautiful, the description of God's enemy (Lucifer).

TWO - Thou shalt not make unto thee any graven image. The image that Christianity has indoctrinated our minds with is past the stage of being graven, it is a direct confrontation with God.

THREE - Thou shalt not bow down thyself to them, or serve them. For I the Lord thy God am a jealous God. Need I say more. Just take a look at the altar of a Christian church, from the Catholic to the black spiritual. It is never built like the altar of God, even though they claim they are worshipping God. The cross, the white Jesus, and his white mother do not belong at the altar of God.

FOUR - Thou shalt not take the name of the Lord thy God in vain. This is the most protected of all the commandments. For very few know His name, and those that are given it in spirit, find it difficult sometimes to understand it, much less to call it in vain. For those that shout Lord, Lord, are not calling His name, for His name is mysterious, for there are many lords and gods, but He is the Lord of Lords and Almighty over all gods. For they are indeed many.

I Corinthians 8:5 "For though they be that are called gods, whether in heaven or in earth, as there be gods many and lords many." So to call on the true and living God must be the **God of our Fathers; the God of Abraham, the God of Isaac, and the God of Israel, for He is the God that liveth in truth**. Nevertheless they, the Christian teachers still lead you to believe, that you are calling on the creator of all things, which is a lie, and a sin within itself.

FIVE - Remember the Sabbath day to keep it holy. Six days thou shalt labour, and do all thy work. But the seventh day is the Sabbath of the Lord thy God, in it thou shalt not do any work, thou nor thy sons, nor thy daughters, thy manservant, nor thy maidservant, nor thy cattle, nor thy stranger that is within thy gates. Since this is where our chapter begins, let's just stop here for awhile.

All these are found in Exodus 20.

Let's see now what Christianity has done to this commandment. First of all, the sabbath is the seventh day, according to the scriptures, unlike some Christian teachers, who tell you that you should give Him one day, any day. The scriptures are written with specific instructions about all of God's laws including His Sabbath.

For we will read in Mark 16:1-2: "And when the SABBATH WAS PAST, Mary Magdalene, and Mary, mother of James, and Salome, had brought sweet spices, that they might come and anoint him. And very early in the morning, the first day of the week, they came unto the sepulchre at the rising of the sun." This scripture did not say any day, it says after the sabbath, and on the first day. How can Christians keep Sunday as though it was the Sabbath, even if it was the Sabbath, how can they then celebrate the same Sunday as the first day, isn't this hypocritical? If Sunday is the first day, then the last day must be the seventh day, **SATURDAY** or the Sabbath.

Now that I have made my point, let's see how the gods of the Christian church changed the law of the Almighty God. Let me take the time to remind you that this pagan religion you know today as Christianity came out of Rome, and started not with God's people, but with Gentiles and strangers.

Romans 11:13 "For I speak to you Gentiles." This is Paul addressing the church of Rome. Let's not forget that the importation was nothing like the exportation of Christianity, and when it was exported God had nothing to do with it, and it had nothing to do with God. For all Romans were worshippers of the sun gods. The emblem of the sun that you find in some Christian churches today started back then on coins, buildings, and things of importance to the state, even the emperors. Sundays were always celebrated as a holiday in Rome, and it was always traditional to serve the sun god on his day, that was named after him.

The first law was passed by the ruler Constantine, making Sunday the official day of worship. This law was passed on March 7, 321 A.D. Note again here that in 321 A.D. Constantine was still a pagan, but wanted everyone to believe that he had changed.

70

The church followed the lead of this pagan Constantine. In the year 325 A.D. SYLVESTER, Bishop of Rome officially called Sunday **the Lord's day** on instruction from the emperor. This happened at the Council of Laodicea.

In 364 A.D. the law was passed that all people must work on Saturdays and no religious services should be carried out. This was decided at the other Council of Laodicea held in that year. So began the philosophy of man.

In Genesis 2:3: "And God blessed the seventh day, and sanctified it, because that in it he had rested from all his work, which God created and made." To sanctify means to set apart, to be different, to be free from the contamination of sin. Jesus said in John 14:15: "If ye love me, keep my commandments." Isn't the Sabbath a commandment of God for you to keep holy? Instead Christianity claims that it is not important, yet, they read the same book of laws, and pay homage to false gods.

Isaiah 8:20: "To the law, and to the testimony they speak not according to the word, it is because there is no light in them." Not forgetting too, that they use the Lord's day to handle, and to bury their dead. They even take the dead to their altar on this day.

I John 2:4: "He that saith, I know him, and keepeth not his commandments is a liar, and the truth is not in him." For in verse 3 is where your strength should be.

I John 2:3: "And hereby we do know, that we know him, if we keep his commandments." That commandment is the Sabbath. There have been no changes from the time the Sabbath had been established by God Himself. Even the Romans call Saturday "SABATO" meaning Sabbath.

Jesus, Himself, showed by example, which was the true day of worship

Luke 4:16: "And he came to Nazareth, where he had been brought up, and as his custom was he went into the synagogue on the Sabbath day, and stood up for to read." Now if the man you claim you serve, worshipped on sabbath, and He came to teach you His way, why then would you disobey?

Luke 4:31: "And came down to Capernaum a city of Galilee, and taught them on the Sabbath days." Look around you and see who are against Sunday shopping? They are of the Christian church. They still call Sunday, the Lord's day. Which Lord?

71

In order to lie effectively Christian leaders write supportive books on their beliefs. They in turn quote their own books making it appear as hidden, but true. They mix the lie with the truth, refer to the lie, then support one pound of that lie with an ounce of truth.

A perfect example would be "The Lost Books of the Bible and The Forgotten Books of Eden." In this book you will discover your ounce of truth mixed with tons of lies. Here are two examples of the lies.

They were so wrapped up in trying to find the answer for the existence of Cain's wife that they created twin sisters for both Cain and Abel. This time they were not smart enough. Page 62 of the story of Adam and Eve, chapter IV verse 3-4 reads: "And God said to Adam; Look at this devil and at his hideous look, and know that he it is who made thee fall from brightness into darkness, from peace and rest to toil and misery. And look O Adam at him who said of himself that he is God. **CAN GOD BE BLACK?"** Let's now deal with this phrase, or verse, or whatever you choose to call it. The holy bible describes God and His people as black with woolly hair and describes Lucifer as fair and beautiful. This is what the Christians read, but what you have just read in "The Forgotten Books of Eden" is what they would want you to believe. Isn't this hypocrisy?

The other lie on page 48 <u>verse 20</u> reads: "Then Adam said to Eve with joy of heart, because of the offering they had made to God, and that had been accepted of Him; Let us do this three times every week. ON THE FOURTH DAY, WEDNESDAY, ON THE PREPARATION DAY, FRIDAY AND ON THE SABBATH, SUNDAY all the days of our lives." If the fourth day is Wednesday, then the first day must be Sunday. If the preparation day is Friday, then the Sabbath must be Saturday. Again the hypocrisy and lies - Christian teachers making themselves gods and changing the laws of God Almighty.

The Lord spoke about these prophets of doom like Constantine, the father of modern Christianity, who claimed to have had visions and dreams of this evil thing. God was concerned about the impact these prophets would have on His children. <u>Jeremiah 23:30-32</u>. "Therefore, behold, I am against the prophets, saith the Lord, that STEAL MY WORDS every one from his neighbour.

Behold, I am against the Prophets, saith the Lord, that use their tongues, and say, HE SAITH. Behold, I am against them that prophesy false dreams, saith the Lord, and do tell them, and cause my people to err by their lies, and by their LIGHTNESS; YET I sent them not, nor commanded them; therefore they shall not profit this people at all, saith the Lord."

BELIEVE IT OR NOT dumb or devout Christians, the time will come when this truth will cut you to pieces like a two edged sword.

WINE IS WRONG

This is one chapter I wish I didn't have to print, but today the times are getting more and more critical, and something must be done, and somebody has to do it. All the prophets from Moses to Jesus, had to warn the children of Israel. They had to teach them about TRUTH, they had to find a way to let the people know, that the things they were doing were wrong, but more than that, they had to live with the aftermath of it. Some of them died from grief, some died at the hands of the enemy, while some died at the hands of their own people. My message is NOT AGAINST BLACK CHRISTIANS, but against the practising of Christianity BY BLACK PEOPLE, which I need for you to examine as we go along. If you should find me wrong, don't just get mad at me, or hate me, BUT PROVE ME WRONG THROUGH THE SCRIPTURES, and I will acknowledge it. I am not here just to criticize, I am here because I have a job to do, and a message to deliver to my people, in the name of the God of our fathers; THE GOD OF ABRAHAM, THE GOD OF ISAAC, AND THE GOD OF JACOB.

If we should analyze everything about Christianity, all that would ever remain would be naught. Here is another lie. Talk to any Christian that claims to be born-again, and communion would be the source of their faith or belief. This communion is taken every one, two, or three months, according to the church's law. Note, not God's law as they claim, but the church's.

We will prove first, that communion is not a religious service and the drinking of wine or grape juice, as some Christians call it, is an abomination to the laws of God and I mean the Almighty God; The God of Abraham, the God of Isaac, and the God of Jacob (ISRAEL). Communion comes from the word commune and commune is one with communicate. The following scriptures tell of the communication of God and His people, the children of Israel. It was the sacrifice at the altar, then later on, we will prove that the method of cup and bread is a means to communicate with God, and not a service within itself. Passover is the law given by God to the hand of Moses, for the children of Israel to obey. This should be kept once a year in the month of Abib.

Exodus 25:22 states: "And there I will meet with thee, and I will COMMUNE with thee, from above the mercy seat, from between the two cherubims, which are upon the Ark of Testimony of all things which I will give thee, in commandment unto the children of Israel." This writing described the word "commune" as dialogue between God and His people.

Let's go now to the next stage of this Christian misconception. I Corinthians 10:16-18: "The cup of blessing, which we bless, is it not the communion of the blood of Christ? The bread which we break, is it not the communion of the body of Christ? For we being many are one bread, and one body. For we are all partakers of that one bread." The above scripture explains that the cup and the bread is that which we communicate with according to law. The eighteenth verse explains who we are: "Behold ISRAEL after the flesh, are not they which eat of the sacrifices partakers of the altar?" This law was given to the children of Israel in the days of Moses. Paul is trying to say here as in the old days, when they killed and sacrificed the lamb, that they were partakers of the altar. In his day it was the bread and the cup, which is the same law of the Passover.

Similar statements were made by Jesus in Luke 22:19: "And he took bread, and gave thanks and brake it, and gave unto them, saying, This is my body which is given for you, this do in remembrance of me." Please note that the twelve disciples were meant to be representative of the twelve tribes of Israel, taught the way of the Israelites, which is to keep the Passover every year, and Jesus is saying that when they keep it, they will remember Him, because it was during Passover when the Romans sought to kill Him. The same words were uttered by God to Moses telling the children of Israel to keep the Passover often, meaning every year in the month of Abib. Exodus 12:14-27 states: "And this day shall be unto you for a MEMORIAL; and ye shall keep it a feast to the Lord THROUGHOUT YOUR GENERATIONS, ye shall keep it a feast by an ordinance FOREVER."

I am sure that if you look up the word "memorial," you will find the meaning being to preserve, to repeat annually, to remember, etc. To confirm this statement given to Moses by God read verse 26: "And it shall come to pass, when your children shall say unto you, what mean ye by this service, And ye shall say, it is the sacrifice of the Lord's Passover. Who passed over

75

the houses of the children of Israel in Egypt, when he smote the Egyptians and delivered our houses." If you were following the scripture, you will find the reason for the Passover. The only difference here is that God delivered the children of Israel from the Egyptians in the month of Abib, and not every Sunday as the Christians would want you to believe.

There is no evidence nor scriptures to prove that you should drink wine or keep what you call communion more than once a year. We have proven that you keep the Passover only once a year, but there is so much more to prove. Christians claim that the Passover, or Last Supper as they will prefer to call it, finished when Jesus died. My dear reader, it was JESUS' last supper, not the last Passover. If this was the case how then did they capture Peter long after the death of Jesus on the Feast of the Unleavened Bread (which is the other name for Passover)? Acts 12:3 says: "And because he saw it pleased the Jews, he proceeded further to take Peter also. Then were the days of unleavened bread." Around this same time the Romans celebrated their pagan festival, to the goddess of spring, Easter. Passover must be kept every year in the month of Abib.

Now let's see what was in the cup to represent blood. In this case the blood of the lamb (Jesus). First, I will prove that the heathens were drinking wine long before Jesus came, and they weren't only drinking wine, they were drinking it at their altar of their god, not the true and living God, but a false god. So remember every time you drink your wine at the altar of damnation, you are drinking the wine of false gods. Amos 2:8 states: "And they lay themselves down upon clothes, laid to pledge by every altar, and they drink the wine of the condemned in the house of their god."

It is very clear what the word of God is saying, it is separating Himself from those who take wine to their altar. For in the days of Amos, Jesus was not yet born. The same is true further back, before Amos. What about in the days of Aaron? Leviticus 10:9-11 says: "Do not drink wine nor strong drink, thou nor thy sons with thee, **when ye go into the Tabernacle** of the Congregation, lest ye die, it shall be a statue FOREVER throughout your GENERATIONS. And that ye may put difference between holy and unholy and between unclean and clean. And that ye may teach the children of Israel all the statues which the Lord hath spoken

76

unto them by the hand of Moses." If you do not understand what is written down here, then no one can help you. To take wine at the altar is unholy and unclean. This is the law and statute given to Moses for the children of Israel by God Himself. For Isaiah says when you prepare a spiritual table with wine that it can never be clean. As a matter of fact it is so unclean that it has been referred to as vomit. Isaiah 28:7-8: "But they also have erred through wine, and through strong drink are out of the way; the priest and the prophet have erred through strong drink; they are swallowed up of wine, they are out of the way through strong drink, they err in vision, they stumble in judgment. For all tables are full of vomit, and filthiness, so that there is no place clean."

Christians march to their churches, taking up their wine every Sunday or whenever, and trying to let you believe that they are serving God. You are not even supposed to keep the Passover in a church of God. God never said for you to keep the Passover in a tabernacle, neither did Jesus. It was Paul who said not to - the same man who Christians claim was a model Christian, when he was not. Paul was an Israelite. ROMANS 11:1 "I say then, hath God cast away his people? I ALSO AM AN ISRAELITE, of the seed of Abraham, of the tribe of Benjamin." Christians can't even follow their own laws, so how can they follow God's? I Corinthians 11:20-22: "When ye come together therefore into one place, this is not to eat the Lord's supper. For in eating every one taketh before other his own supper: and one is hungry, and another is drunken. What? have ye not houses to eat and to drink in? or despise ye the church of God, and shame them that have not? What shall I say to you? shall I praise you in this? I PRAISE YOU NOT."

Again this Israelite is trying to teach pagans to no avail. What is happening in the Christian church today? Mind you there is no law stating that you should not drink wine, except in church. The Christians say, don't drink it at all, only drink it in church. What does the bible say to that. Let's read I Timothy 5:34 **"Drink no longer water, but use a little wine for thy stomach's sake, and thine often infirmities."**

According to the scriptures, you drink wine for your sickness, your infirmities, for your bad stomach, not for the work of God. You must remember that Jesus Himself made wine at the wedding

77

party, but never is it written in any true word of God that wine is even close to the services of God. For the fury of God being so enraged, you can almost reach out and touch His anger when you read Jeremiah 25:15-16: "For thus saith the Lord God of Israel unto me; Take the wine cup of this fury at my hand, and cause all the nations to whom I send thee, to drink it. And they shall drink, and be moved, and be mad, because of the sword that I will send among them." This is how mad the Almighty Father is at His people for drinking wine in His house. Now is the time for you to take a good look at yourself, to see if that curse doesn't apply to black people of the Americas today, the descendants of the Israelites. All I'm asking for, is honesty.

Let's now take a peep in the cup from which Jesus and the disciples drank. Let's look for the contents of that cup. Before we peep in, I will tell you. IT WAS WATER, not wine. Now let's prove it. Mark 14:12-14: "And the first day of unleavened bread, when they killed the Passover, his disciples said unto him, where wilt thou that we go and prepare, that thou mayest eat the Passover. And He sendeth forth two of his disciples, and saith unto them, go ye into the city and there shall meet you a man, bearing a pitcher of **water,** follow him. And wheresoever he may go in, say ye to the good man of the house. The master saith, where is the guest chamber. Where I shall eat the Passover with my disciples." You may also read this, in Luke 22.

Two things have been learnt here. First, to prepare for the Passover you need the first firmament: **water.** Secondly, you keep the Passover in a house or home, not a church. Let's read Luke 22:18: "For I say unto you, I will not drink of the fruit of the vine, until the kingdom of God shall come." Christians use this sentence claiming the FRUIT OF THE VINE can only mean wine, but it is not. The answer is in John 15:1 "I am the true vine, and my father the husbandman." Let me try to explain. The meaning of husbandman is that of a farmer. One that tills the soil, nourishes the seed and cares for the plant. In other words Jesus is telling them that He is nothing, just a vine. It is the spirit within Him that is His father, for it is the spirit that quickeneth the body. Jesus represented flesh, while the Christ represents the Spirit that He so often turned to.

Let's see what is the fruit of the spirit in Galations 5:22: "But the fruit of the spirit is love, joy, peace, long suffering,

78

gentleness, goodness, faith." So far nothing about wine. This is the spiritual explanation of the fruit of the vine. Let's look at the physical. I Corinthians 11:25 states: "After the same manner also he took the CUP, when he had supped saying, This cup is the New Testament in my BLOOD. This do ye as oft as ye drink it in remembrance of me." We would now have to prove what was in His blood, and the answer is in John 19:34: "But one of the soldiers with a spear pierced his side and forth with came there out **blood and WATER.**"

Let's continue to show through the scriptures the significance of bread and water, and that water is indeed the true representation of blood, and that there can be no other substitute for blood other than water. It could not have been wine, because along with the evils of wine, it is not original. It was water that Jesus took, to make wine, how then can wine represent the blood of Jesus the Christ?

WATER AND BLOOD

EXODUS 7:17: "Thus saith the Lord, in this thou shalt know, that I am the Lord, behold I will smite with the rod, that is in mine hand, upon the WATERS which are in the river and they shall be turned into BLOOD." Exodus 4:9: "And it shall come to pass, if they will not believe also these two signs neither hearken unto thy voice, that thou shalt take of the WATER of the river, and pour it upon the dry land, and the WATER which thou takest out of the river, shall become BLOOD upon the dry land." Revelations 8:8. "And the second angel sounded and as it were a great mountain, burning with fire, was cast into the sea, and the third part of the sea became BLOOD." Revelation 16:4: "And the third angel poured out his vial upon the rivers, and fountains of WATER, and they became BLOOD."

Now that we have proven with all these scriptures how important water is, let me explain something else to you. Do you know that man cannot make raw materials? Everything we enjoy upon this earth, comes from something of the earth, planted here by God, Himself. This goes for WATER. Water was the first firmament before God created the earth. That makes it the first of all raw materials. It flows, it causes man and beast to live, every living thing that is upon the earth, would not have been upon the earth hadn't it been for water. Water is the source of all creation. Man can make wine, but only God can make water.

Let's prove it with the scriptures. Genesis 1:2: "And the earth was without form, and void, and darkness was upon the face of the DEEP. And the Spirit of God moved upon the face of the WATERS." Verse 6-10 reads. "And God said, Let there be a firmament in the midst of the WATERS, and let it divide the WATERS from the WATERS.

And God made the firmament. And divide the WATERS which were under the firmament from the WATERS which were above the firmament: and it was so.

And God called the firmament Heaven. And the evening and the morning were the second day.

And God said, Let the WATERS under the heaven be gathered together unto one place, and let the dry land appear: and it was so.

And God called the dry land Earth; and the gathering together of the WATERS called the Seas; and God saw that it was good."

We have read where it is stated in the scriptures that water was the very foundation of creation. Why then are you using wine? If water is such a powerful element to God why then would Jesus chose wine for spiritual communication over water? when He Himself took water and made wine for His first miracle. John 2:7-9: "Jesus saith unto them, Fill the water pots with WATER. And they filled them up to the brim. And he said unto them, Draw out now and bear into the governor of the feast. And they bare it. When the ruler of the feast had tasted the WATER that was made wine, and knew not whence it was." If we should read verse 11 it tells you that this was the first miracle by Jesus. "This beginning of miracles did Jesus in Cana of Galilee." Again it was the first, and again it was with WATER.

Let's continue to read what the bible says about the pagans, who used wine for their spiritual works that even the children of Israel believed in. Just like the Christians today believe that the wine they are drinking for communion is the right thing.

Isaiah 51:17: "Awake, awake, stand up O Jerusalem which hast drunk at the hand of the Lord, the cup of his fury. Thou hast drunken the dregs of the cup of trembling and wrung them out."

Let's go to another scripture to find out (1) What is the "DREGS"

(2) whether it is accepted by God or rejected. Psalm 75:8: "For in the hand of the Lord there is a cup, and the wine is red, it is full of mixture; and he poureth out of the same, but the DREGS thereof, all the wicked of the earth shall wring them out and drink them." Jeremiah 49:12: "For thus saith the Lord, Behold they whose judgment, was not to drink of the cup have assuredly drunken: and art thou he that shall altogether go unpunished? Thou shalt not go unpunished, but thou shalt surely drink of it."

Knowing how hard it is for Christians to absorb truth, it will be difficult for them to see the power of water. Bearing in mind, that JESUS walked on it, did almost every miracle with, or by it, including the areas where He performed miracles, and it was always by rivers or wells. Your memory might not serve you well so here are some scriptures to support these facts which are TRUTH.

Ezekiel 31:16: "I made the nations to shake at the sound of his fall, when I cast him down to hell, with them that descend into the pit, and all the trees of Eden, the choice and best of Lebanon. All that drink WATER shall be comforted in the nether parts of the earth." The above scripture is telling us that even in the midst of the destruction of Lucifer who was cast down to the pit and is raging mad, those of us who take WATER shall be comforted.

Let's now go to the New Testament and find the power of water there as well. John 5:3-4 "In these lay a great multitude of impotent folk, of blind, halt, withered, waiting for the moving of the WATER. For an angel went down at a certain season into the pool, and troubled the WATER, whosoever then first after the troubling of the water stepped in was made whole of whatsoever disease he had." Some people, Christians in particular, believe that the juice of the grape is not wine. I find it so difficult to believe that grown-ups believe this lie. Don't we know that it is the juice of the grape that makes wine, and vinegar? Therefore, if this so-called juice is not wine, then vinegar is not wine either. It is so much against God's law to use any of these things in His name, that when He cried out for WATER on the cross, they gave Him the opposite: Vinegar. This is like saying "I don't eat pork, but I eat ham, or bacon." They are all from the same cursed animal.

That's why I'm trying so hard to let you see the light. It is not a sin to drink wine, but you shouldn't use it on God's Sabbath, at

His altar, during prayers, and when calling upon His name. You should not mix wine with the works of God, for it is unclean. I Peter 4:7: "But the end of all things is at hand, be ye therefore sober, and watch unto prayer."

Let's now prove that wine that comes from the grapes that comes from the vine are all unclean for God's work. This makes your so-called grape juice sinful. Numbers 6:3: "He shall separate himself from wine, and strong drink and shall drink no vinegar of wine or vinegar of strong drink, neither shall he drink any liquor of grapes, nor eat moist grapes or dried." Judges 13:14: "She may not eat of anything that cometh of the vine, neither let her drink wine or strong drink, nor eat any unclean thing all that I commanded her, let her observe."

Read Numbers 6:2. It tells you clearly of the separation. "Speak unto the children of Israel, and say unto them. When either man or woman shall separate themselves to vow a vow of a Nazarite, to separate themselves unto the Lord." There is still more proof. This time about Elijah (John the Baptist). Luke 1:15. "For he shall be great in the sight of the Lord, and shall drink neither wine nor strong drink, and he shall be filled with the Holy Ghost even from his mother's womb." Because he was filled with the Holy Ghost he was not allowed to drink wine. So how is it when members of the church want the spirit, they drink wine? Now ask yourself whose spirit and what spirit?

Let's close this chapter reading Mark 9:41: "For whosoever shall give you a cup of water to drink in my name because ye belong to Christ. Verily I say unto you, he shall not lose his reward." If you must make contact with God, do it the right way. Because the Amonites and Moabites did not meet the children of Israel with BREAD and WATER, God said they shall not enter into the congregation of the Lord. Duet. 23:4: "Because they met you not with bread and with water in the way when ye came forth out of Egypt..." To find out what was the method used by Samuel to communicate with God, read I Samuel 7:6: "And they gathered together to Mizpeh, and drew WATER and poured it out before the Lord, and fasted on that day and said there, we have sinned against the Lord, and Samuel judged the children of Israel in Mizpeh." Isaiah 3:1: " For behold the Lord, the Lord of hosts, doth take away from Jerusalem, and from Judah the stay, and staff, the whole stay of BREAD, and the whole stay of WATER."

If wine was indeed holy, why did Jesus refuse it after they took Him, and another black man Simon to a place of the dead and gave Him wine? Mark 15:21-23: "And they compelled one Simon, a Cyrenian, who passed by coming out of the country, the father of Alexander and Rufus to bear his cross. And they bring him, unto the place Golgotha, which is being interpreted, the place of a skull. And they gave him to drink WINE mingled with myrrh, but he received it not." Note, they did everything to Him, that was against His teachings. First, they took Him to a place of the dead, then they gave Him wine, but He refused it. These two black men were placed in a time of turmoil. Cyrene is the other name for Libya, which is in North Africa.

Relax, and let's read together and analyze. Leviticus 23:10 -13 "Speak unto the children of Israel, and say unto them, When ye be come into the LAND which I give unto you, and shall reap the HARVEST thereof, then ye shall bring a sheaf of the first fruits of your harvest unto the priest:

And he shall wave the sheaf before the Lord, to be accepted for you: on the morrow AFTER THE SABBATH the priest shall wave it.

And ye shall offer that day when ye wave the sheaf an he lamb without blemish of the first year for a burnt offering unto the Lord.

And the meat offering thereof shall be two tenth deals of fine flour mingled with oil, an offering made by fire unto the Lord for a sweet savour: and the drink offering thereof shall be of WINE, the fourth part of an hin."

Two things must be made very clear. (1) Our fathers drank wine in celebration of their harvest, in other words, they celebrated the gift of the land. (2) This celebration was never kept on the Sabbath, if you notice carefully you would find that it was AFTER THE SABBATH. There is still more, if you read with me again, you will discover that there were three feasts in the year, that our fathers kept for the Lord. (1) Feast of Unleavened Bread; Passover. (2) Feast of the Tabernacle; Day of Atonement. (3) Feast of the land.

We have lost the right to celebrate the third feast, since we now lost the Land of Milk and Honey, that is now occupied by Edomites calling themselves Jews. This was predicted in the words of Malachi.

MALACHI 1:4 "Whereas EDOM saith; We are impoverished, but we will return and build the desolate places; thus saith the Lord of hosts; They shall build, but I will throw down; and they shall call them, the border of wickedness, and, the people against whom the Lord hath indignation for ever." That leaves us with the first two feasts. EXODUS 23:14 "Three times thou shalt keep a feast unto me in the year."

Again let me remind you that the Passover is not the same as communion. **COMMUNION IS WRONG** it does not represent anything pertaining to GOD. PASSOVER IS RIGHT it is an ordinance given by God Himself. The first law God gave to our father Moses. It should be kept with water, in a home, and not every Sunday, but every year.

Exodus 13:10 "Thou shalt therefore keep this **ORDINANCE** in his season **FROM YEAR TO YEAR**."

These are the laws given to our father Moses by our Almighty Father God Himself. Ask yourself, whose laws are you living by from day to day. No wonder we are suffering the way we are. We are disobedient children and are being punished by the God of our fathers.

Here is another scripture used by desperate Christians to justify their using of wine in their church. ISAIAH 65:8 "Thus saith the Lord, as the new wine is found in the cluster, and one saith destroy it not: for a blessing is in it; so will I do for my servants sakes, that I may not destroy them all."

Any intelligent person should be able to understand what is written here. When new wine is in the cluster, it is not destroyed. This is symbolic to the children of God. They are **like** the new wine. "I will not destroy my servants saith the Lord once the new wine is within them." The new wine is "**THE TRUTH**." It has nothing to do with the drinking of wine.

When Daniel spoke to the Angel of God, he stayed away from wine, when the Christians want the spirit they take wine. Daniel 10: 3 " I ate no pleasant bread,neither came flesh **nor wine in my mouth,** neither did I anoint myself at all, till three whole weeks were fulfilled".

Please feel free to use your wine at your church on your altar, but remember, I warned you of its consequences. I am not trying to change anyone, but hope that everyone changes from the evils of this pagan practice.

BODY SOUL AND SPIRIT

This chapter will be a very difficult one, for there are so many ways to explain these dimensions. Understanding of all its contents would not come easy, but let us try anyway.

BODY: Flesh, bones, marrow, blood, etc.

OTHER TERM: Physical.

SOUL: Inner self-being, unseen.

OTHER TERM: Mind or conscience.

SPIRIT: Inner being, unseen by the naked eye, a being that can survive outside a body, can appear as flesh. Some are known only by the Almighty Spirit. This dimension can be controlled by other spirits in man. It is the force that exercises the senses in man, and can survive after the death of the original body.

OTHER TERM: Ghost.

Let's examine an every day exercise that we all take for granted, something the physical world is still trying to come to grips with. DREAMING: How we dream, what happens when we dream, and how is it connected to the three dimensions of MAN.

In the days of old, when men were wiser, and more knowledgeable about spiritual things, dreams were important to them. It was through dreams that men communicated with the unseen. It was through dreams, that God communicated with His people. It was through dreams that the children of Israel were saved.

How does one dream? You would have noticed that both soul and spirit are unseen. Later in this chapter you will also discover that they both reside in your body (flesh). Within the framework of your complete being, there is no better communicating link than with these two dimensions. To put it in a more simple form, is to say that the spirit goes out and encounters activities, then reports back to the soul, which is responsible for the decision making.

Spiritual things can only be seen by the spiritual eye, so in order to communicate with the inner you, it must be done with the spirit. For instance, if God wants to talk to man, He would usually put him in a deep sleep, then He would talk to his spirit, because He is spirit. The spirit would then convey the message to the soul which is your individual representative. The soul would now highlight your awareness in the decision making process.

You cannot have more than one soul in your body, because it is the soul that will answer long after your body has been destroyed, but you can have more than one spirit within your body, beside your own. These spirits are called adopted spirits, and adopted spirits are called entities.

We will now turn to the scriptures for the importance of dreams. The following came out of the mouth of the Almighty God Himself, talking to Miriam and Aaron.

Numbers 12:6 "And he said, Hear now my words; if there be a prophet among you, I the Lord will make myself known unto him in a VISION AND WILL SPEAK UNTO HIM IN A DREAM."

I Kings 3:5 "In Gideon the Lord appeared to Solomon in a DREAM by night; and God said, ask what I shall give thee."

The next piece of scripture might be a little plainer for all to understand. Job 33:14-17 "For God speaketh once, yea twice, yet man perceiveth it not. In a DREAM, in a vision of the night, when deep sleep falleth upon men in slumberings upon the bed: Then he openeth the ears of men, and sealeth their instruction. That he may withdraw man from his purpose, and hide pride from man."

The last few verses reveal the purpose and importance of dreams. Yet if one does not understand fully, they can mistake evil dreams for holy messages.

There are some people that cannot dream about anything positive, cannot dream of holy things, such as streams of cool clear water, or lovely green pastures full of flowers with streams and brooks. They can never dream of stairways and hills, only pits and darkness, muddy waters and evil. This is typical of people who live evil lives. If your life is evil, your surroundings will be evil, your dreams would be evil, for the good spirit cannot communicate with, or dwell in an unclean vessel. If the spirit is unclean, then so is the vessel. (body). They both look after their own. The earthbound adopted spirits, that is not of God, are being mistaken most times for the spirit of God.

The bible also speaks of two very important times in the history of the children of Israel, whereby they were saved through the interpretation of dreams. One was with Joseph.

86

Genesis 37:5 "And Joseph dreamed a dream, and he told it to his brethren; and they hated him yet the more." If you continue to read further, you will find out why, but let's see how it would involve all Israel. If you read Genesis 40 & 41 it will tell you the story of Joseph interpreting the dreams that saved the children of Israel and the great country of Egypt.

The other is Daniel. Daniel 4 & 5 is yet another demonstration of the importance of dreams. There are countless stories of dreams in the bible, but our topic really is about body, soul and spirit. Let's try to put them together in the context of the Supreme Judge.

FATHER - SON - AND - HOLY GHOST

FATHER: SPIRIT. (THE CHRIST)

SON: BODY (JESUS)

HOLYGHOST: UNISON OF SPIRITUAL FORCES, THE COMFORTER, (TRUTH).

God is Father, Son and Holy Ghost - not God the Father, God the Son, and God the Holy Ghost. The latter are three gods, and the bible teaches us of only one God, the Almighty One.

Therefore, you might ask, who is Jesus? Is He the Son of God? Does He have a heavenly mother? NO! How can a man be a man, and be a god, or God? You will find it all very confusing without the spirit of understanding. This is where the teachers of false philosophies trap the inquiring mind, for answers can seem very convincing on either side. You would find that some teachers who believe that Jesus is God, might be able to prove it to you, likewise those who do not believe that He was God on earth, can convince you, through scriptures they read also.

I have also listened and read about the dimensions of man. I am always bombarded from both sides. Some do not believe in body, soul, and spirit. They claim that your body is your soul, while some believe that man is made up of body, that is separate from your soul, and from your spirit.

Let's try now to examine all the scriptures to find the truth, and to find that truth we would have to go back to the very beginning when God said in Genesis 1:26 "And God said, let us make man in our image, after our likeness..." Reading this scripture and looking at man today will make one wonder, was God really like man? The answer is God made man like Himself. This can also be confirmed in I Corinthians 15:44.

87

"It is sown a natural body, it is raised a spiritual body. There is a natural body, and there is a spiritual body." Please read to the 46th verse, then check for more information in the second chapter of this book, "The First Family." There you will learn that they were all men. After the impurities that inflicted the first terrestrial family, infirmities which made them unclean and blemished in the presence of God, He (God) took on the permanent stage of a spiritual form. According to the scriptures God was now a spirit. You may then ask what Jesus has to do with all this, for He was flesh and bones and God is a spirit.

Before I prove or explain this, I will have to prove how three is one and the body, soul and spirit are all separate one from another. Then I'll have to prove that there is only one God. Then you might be able to come to your own conclusion. Hebrews 4:12 states: "For the word of God is quick and powerful and sharper than any two edged sword, piercing even to the dividing asunder **of soul, and spirit,** and of the JOINTS and MARROW and is a discerner of the thoughts and intents of the heart." Joints and marrow in the above scripture means flesh or body, for it is your body that is made up of joints and the marrow is between the joints. This explanation is in Matthew 10:28: "And fear not them, which kill the body, but are not able to kill the SOUL, but rather fear him which is able to destroy both SOUL and BODY in hell." The above confirms the meaning of joints and marrow for the word body is being used here.

Let's see how Job describes this. Job 14:22: "But his flesh upon him, shall have pain and his SOUL within him shall mourn." II Kings 4:27: "And when she came to the man of God, to the hill, she caught him by the feet, but Gehazi came near to thrust her away. And the man of God said, let her alone, for her SOUL is vexed WITHIN HER."

Let's continue to prove that your soul and your spirit is within your body. James 2:26 states: "For as the BODY without the SPIRIT is dead, so faith without works is dead also." I Kings 17:21-22: "And he stretched himself upon the child three times, and cried unto the Lord, and said O, Lord, my God, I pray thee, let this child's SOUL come into him again. And the Lord heard the voice of Elijah and the SOUL of the child came into him again, and he revived."

To those Christian teachers who try so hard to prove that your body is your soul read scriptures like <u>Ezekiel 18:20</u>: "The SOUL that sinneth shall die, the son shall not bear the iniquity of the father, neither shall the father bear the iniquity of the son, the righteousness of the righteous shall be upon him and the wickedness of the wicked shall be upon him." This scripture confirms that the soul is not immortal and that it can die. It does not however, prove that your body is your soul. It also proves that the soul is your individual responsibility - every man is responsible for his own soul. The soul of the father will not suffer because of the sins of the son.

It is only through your reading for yourself, that you would be in a better position to understand God's word, for this is not a book where I tell you what to do, but what is right and what is wrong, a book where you, through your own understanding, make the decision between the truth and the lie. For this is the way the Almighty God intended it to be. That's why He gave Adam and Eve the freedom of the garden, and allowed them the choice of right and wrong. <u>I Thessalonians 5:23</u>: "And the very God of peace sanctify you wholly, and I pray God, your whole SPIRIT and SOUL, and BODY be preserved blameless unto the coming of our Lord Jesus Christ."

I am sure that you would be satisfied after reading the above. Now you know, but let me refresh your memory that God is one and that there is no other REAL God. We will put the pieces together about Jesus and the three in one. <u>James 2:19</u>: "Thou believest that there is one God, thou doest well, the devils also believe and tremble." <u>Duet. 32:39</u>: "See now, that I, even I, am he, and there is no god with me, I kill and I make alive, I wound, and I heal, neither is there any that can deliver out of my hand."

All these messages and statements were given to God's people to acknowledge God as one, for the heathens have more than one god. Please note that for the Israelites there should be no other gods, because it works both ways; for the Almighty God there is no other people, but for all other people to have God they must do the things that are right in the sight of God, and the things that are right are the teachings of the children of Israel, by their God. <u>Isaiah 48:12</u> "Hearken unto me O Jacob and Israel my CALLED, I am he, I am the FIRST, I also am the LAST."

89

So far we have proven, that there is body, soul, and spirit, and there is only one God. Now we must prove the connection with Jesus to all this. John 1:1-10 "In the beginning was the word and the word was with God, and the word was God." First there is a separation, then there is the unison. "The word was with God" means the word is unseen, and so is the spirit, the spirit was with God. Next "The word was God." The person within whom the spirit resides is made whole. To sum this up is to confirm that God, of whom we read about in "The First Family" was like unto man in spirit form, meaning CELESTIAL.

Let's go on. "The same was in the beginning WITH God." Again separation, with God meaning along with God, and celestial being heavenly or spiritual flesh that can be separated in its highest forms and put together if need be, by God Himself. Verse 3: "All things were made by him, and without him, was not anything made, that was made." We read in the writings of Moses in Deuteronomy 32:39: and in Isaiah 45:12: "I have made the earth, and created man upon it, I, even my hands have stretched out the heavens, and all their hosts, have I commanded." These are almost identical words used by John and Moses, but we can sum it all up if we read John 1:10: "He was in the world, and the world was made by him, and the world knew him not."

What we are discovering here, is that this supreme being we know as God, was in the world, and the world did not know Him. Because of this mystery of God, and Son, we continue to have legitimate arguments on both sides. The people who believe that God and Jesus are separate do not believe in body, soul and spirit.

Since we have proven this, let's continue to look at the separation of Jesus and God and the unison. Revelation 5:1-6. "And I saw in the right hand of him that sat on the throne, a book written within and on the backside sealed with seven seals. And I saw a strong angel, proclaiming with a loud voice. Who is worthy to open the book, and to loose the seals thereof?" and verse 6 says, "And I beheld, and lo, in the midst of the throne and of the four beasts, and in the midst of the elders stood a Lamb, as it had been slain, having seven horns, and seven eyes, **which are the seven Spirits of God,** sent forth into all the earth." There is the separation again, first the man that sat on the throne with the book that only the lamb, who is Jesus, can open.

Please note the "right hand of Him" being SPIRIT, and lamb being FLESH.

We also learn of the Seven Spirits of God. One or more spirits can speak in the heavens to Jesus and in the eyes of the flesh they seem like a separation, but this had its purpose, for Jesus could not claim to be God, knowing that He was going to die the physical death. Judging from the track record of the Israelites, they would now believe that God is DEAD, and all hopes of the covenant would be lost, the second coming would be irrelevant to all the people, and this is why you must know this truth. John 12:28-30: "Father glorify thy name, then came there a voice from heaven, saying I have both glorified it and will glorify it again. The people therefore, that stood by and heard it, said that it thundered, others said an angel spake to him. Jesus answered and said, **This voice came not because of me, but for your sakes.**" This is living proof of Jesus deliberately separating Himself from the Supreme Being, especially in a crowd among a multitude, but with His disciples He was often diplomatic. John 5:46: "For had ye believed Moses, ye would have believed me, for he wrote of me." He is still not saying He is God, but listen to His statements. John 6:62: "What and if ye shall see the son of man ascend up where he was before?"

Let's study the story of His birth by the prophet Isaiah. Isaiah 7:14: "Therefore the Lord himself shall give you a sign. Behold a virgin shall conceive, and bear a son, and shall call his name Emanuel." The word "Lord" is not only used in the New Testament. Note here it says the "Lord" Himself, meaning that He, **CHRIST** Himself, arranged it all. Isaiah 9:6: "For unto us a child is born, unto us a son is given, and the government shall be upon his shoulders, and his name shall be called, Wonderful, Counsellor, THE MIGHTY GOD, THE EVERLASTING FATHER, The Prince of Peace."

Bear in mind there is only one God who is the everlasting Father and Himself being called both Almighty God, Mighty God and also called Lord in the Old Testament. For David called upon Him in Psalm 50:1: "The Mighty God, even the Lord hath spoken, and called the earth, from the rising of the sun, unto the going down thereof." and we can also prove this in Matthew 1:23: " Behold a virgin shall be with child and shall bring forth a son, and they shall call his name EMMANUEL which being interpreted **is God with us."**

These words are very heavy to people who might want to doubt the word of God and still read it, and preach about it. To them I say be like the Jehovah Witnesses and others that print their own book from the King James version of the bible to teach their own doctrine. Print your own book, only this time call upon another name for your own god.

Let's look at His place of residence before Mary's womb. John 3:13: "And no man hath ascended up to heaven, but he that come down from heaven, even the son of man which is in heaven." The 31st verse: "He that cometh from above, is above all, he that is of the earth is earthly, and speaketh of the earth, he that cometh from heaven is above all." John 1:15 explains that CHRIST was in existence before the miraculous birth of Jesus. Here John the Baptist tells it all: "John bear witness of him and cried saying, this was he of whom I spake, that cometh after me, is prepared before me, for he was before me." John 8:23: "And he said unto them, ye are from beneath, I am from above. Ye are of this world. I am not of this world."

In order for you to see Jesus the Christ as a power on earth, and from above, according to the scriptures, He is saying that He is from above and He is God. Therefore to see Him separate from the Almighty God will be acknowledging two gods. So the scripture in Mark will be difficult for you to understand. Mark 12:29: "And Jesus answered him, the first of all commandments is HEAR, O ISRAEL, THE LORD OUR GOD IS ONE LORD."

Israelites must believe in one God and must believe in the teachings of His holy word. We must look to the scriptures for the truth, and the truth is, there is no difference between the Father, which is the spirit within Jesus, and the celestial flesh of Jesus. John 8:19: "Then said they unto him, where is thy father? Jesus answered, ye neither know me nor my father, if ye had known me, ye should have known my father also." Here continues the relationship between flesh and spirit that are apart, yet uniquely together.

It is summed up best in Colossians 2:9: "For in him dwelleth all the fullness of the Godhead bodily." This means that the spirits of God were in Jesus, for when the spirit took hold, then the acts of God could not have been prevented. With all the carefulness of Jesus, the Spirit or the Christ seeped through. That's why they wanted to stone Him in John 10:32-33.

92

"Jesus answered them, many good works have I shewed you from my father, for which of those works do ye stone me? The Jews answered him saying, for a good work we stone thee not, but for blasphemy and because that thou being a man maketh thyself, God." The Jews could not understand it. They knew that God was a spirit, but they could not understand Him being a man, not even those close to Him. Even Thomas in John 20:28: "And Thomas answered and said unto him my LORD and my GOD." Thus even Thomas acknowledged that the **CHRIST** was God after they had killed the **body of JESUS.**

Philip also was confused by all this. John 14:7-9: "If ye had known me, ye should have known my father also and from henceforth ye know him, and have seen him. Philip said unto him, Lord show us the Father and it sufficeth us. Jesus said unto him, have I been so long time with you, and yet hast thou not known me Philip? He that hath seen me, hath seen the father, and how sayest thou then, show us the Father." For it was Timothy who gave us the best answer to the spiritual question in his description of Jesus or God. I Timothy 3:16: "And without controversy, great is the mystery of godliness, GOD was manifest in the FLESH, justified in the spirit, seen of angels, preached unto the Gentiles, believeth on in the world, RECEIVED UP INTO GLORY." To put it clearer than that is to come right out and say JESUS THE CHRIST is indeed GOD.

Anyhow we still must continue to prove that He was, before His earthly birth. John 8:57-58: "Then said the Jews unto him, thou art not yet fifty years old, and hast thou seen Abraham? Jesus said unto them; Verily verily I say unto you before Abraham was I am." The same goes for David. Read Matthew 22:42-45: "Saying what think ye of Christ? Whose son is he? They say unto him, The Son of David. He saith unto them, How then doth David in spirit called him, Lord, saying. The Lord said unto my Lord, sit thou on my right hand till I make thine enemies thy footstool." If David then called him Lord, how is He his SON? Every time it is proven that He called upon the Father, remember He said that the Father is the husbandman, and the husbandman means the one that makes things happen, the SPIRIT. There is no proof that a body can be separated from the spirit and live. So when Jesus called on the Father it's just the flesh calling on the spirit, and in most cases He had to do it only when there was a crowd, as I mentioned before. You will also begin to realize that there is a difference between Jesus, and the Christ. Jesus was the son of Mary, but THE CHRIST is the God of Abraham, the God of Isaac, and the God of Jacob, and nobody's son. He was, and still is, the everlasting FATHER, AND ALMIGHTY SPIRIT.

Let's take the case of Lazarus. Remember when Jesus raised Lazarus from the dead, He was groaning in the spirit? John 11:33: "When Jesus therefore saw her weeping and the Jews also weeping which came with her, He GROANED in the SPIRIT and was troubled." This is what He said in Verse 42: "And I knew that thou hearest me always, but **because of the people** which stand by I said it, that they may believe that thou hast sent me." Again this is proof that Jesus did not want the people to know who He really was. For He was before Abraham, He is David's Father, and not his son, and He did not have any father nor mother according to the scriptures. Hebrews 7:3: "Without FATHER, without MOTHER, without descent, having neither beginning of days nor end of life, but made like unto the SON OF GOD, abideth a priest continually." He was also the one that led the children of Israel out of the land of Egypt for He was the Rock. Exodus 17:6: "Behold I will stand before thee there upon the rock in Horeb; and thou shalt smite the rock, and there shall come water out of it, that the people may drink and Moses did so in the sight of the elders of Israel." I Samuel 2:2: "There is none Holy as the Lord, for there is none beside thee, neither is there any ROCK like our God."

Deuteronomy 32:4 "He is the Rock, his work is perfect, for all his ways are judgment. A God of truth, and without iniquity, just and right is he." Here God has been identified as strength, solid as a Rock, for he was the Rock, and to know who the Rock was read I Corinthians 10:4: "And did all drink the same spiritual drink, for they drank of that spiritual ROCK, that followed them, and that Rock was Christ."

You will notice that the scripture states, that the rock was Christ and not Jesus, it is very important for the children of God to understand this truth. There is more than one person with the name Jesus. Colossians 4:11 "And JESUS, which is called JUSTUS, who are of the Circumcision. These only are my fellow workers unto the Kingdom of God, which have been a comfort unto me" This scripture is not referring to the Christ, yet the name

94

Jesus is mentioned. THINK ABOUT IT! This Jesus is also of the Circumcision, and also a JEW. JESUS IS FLESH, THE CHRIST IS THE SPIRIT. <u>II Corinthians 11:4</u> "For if he that cometh **preacheth another Jesus...**"

Here is a perfect example, let's just say that you love Jim because he is a good person, how would I know which of the Jims you are talking about? There are three JIMS that I know, Jim Baker, Jim Jones, and Jim Swaggart. How will I know the difference between the KILLER, the LIAR, and the CHEAT? They are all Christians. In order to identify the particular Jim you must describe him.

This is the description of God in <u>Isaiah 52:14</u>: "As many were astonied at thee, his visage was as marred, more than any man, and his form, more than the sons of men." And this is the description of Jesus the Christ in <u>Isaiah 53:2</u>: "For he shall grow up before him as a tender plant, and as a root out of a dry ground, he hath no form, nor comeliness, and when we shall see him, there is no beauty that we should desire him." What do you think? Seems like the same person to me.

WHEN YOU PRAY, PRAY NOT TO JESUS AS YOU HAVE BEEN TAUGHT, BUT TO THE CHRIST, OR JESUS THE CHRIST. FOR CHRIST IS THE SPIRIT OF GOD, THE GOD OF OUR FATHERS; THE GOD OF ABRAHAM, THE GOD OF ISAAC AND THE GOD OF JACOB.

HOW TO PRAY

It would be very frustrating for anyone to be hungry, buy some spaghetti, but have no pot, no fire, and nothing to cook it with. This would be like having no spaghetti. The spaghetti then becomes indeed useless.

There are two types of knowledgeable folks. The one who knows; but never practices, and the other who knows; but can't or won't because of circumstances. It's like reading about faith without works or vice versa, but we are not talking about that. In this chapter we are talking about communing with God, talking to Him, feeling His presence, knowing what to say, knowing what to do, and communication with the Almighty is done through prayer. How do we pray and what do we say?

First of all, let me remind you, that the bible is not a Christian book, it is a book for the children of Israel. Knowing this would help, since you want to pray to the same God as the children of Israel did, I hope! Let's assume that you need to commune with Him, the true God. You first must know the name of which he approved for you to call him by, and how to call upon it.

So let's find out His name, for God is not His name. God is His office, or His title for there are many gods. In the early days He had no name, so He was known as Lord God, then the Almighty God. Then came the children of Israel and His name began to change rapidly, avoiding unclean lips to utter it, and those that were not worthy to call upon it.

Now let's go back to when His name was just simply God, or Lord God, or Lord thy God. Genesis 2: 7: "And the LORD GOD formed man of the dust of the ground, and breathed into his nostrils, the breath of life, and man became a living soul." This was the beginning of all things. He was known here as LORD GOD.

Let's see now how this was changed or added to. Genesis 17:1: "And when Abram was ninety years old and nine, the Lord appeared to Abram and said unto him. I am the ALMIGHTY GOD; walk before me, and be thou perfect." This also was the beginning of the contact with the earthly father and His children. When there was only Abraham in the generation of God, God was known then as the GOD OF HEAVEN.

96

Genesis 24:3: "And I will make thee swear by the Lord, the GOD OF HEAVEN, and the GOD OF THE EARTH."

Then came the story of Joseph in Egypt and in those days God was known as the GOD OF OUR FATHERS by the children of Israel, and also by the GOD OF ABRAHAM. While in the days of Moses, He was known as I AM, and the introduction of His everlasting name, THE GOD OF ABRAHAM, THE GOD OF ISAAC, and THE GOD OF JACOB. Exodus 3:14-15: "And God said unto Moses, I AM that I AM and he said; Thus shalt thou say unto the children of Israel, I AM hath sent me unto you. And God said moreover unto Moses, thus shalt thou say unto the children of Israel, **THE LORD GOD OF YOUR FATHERS. The GOD OF ABRAHAM, THE GOD OF ISAAC, and THE GOD OF JACOB hath sent me unto you. THIS IS MY NAME FOREVER and THIS IS MY MEMORIAL UNTO ALL GENERATIONS."**

We will return to this scripture for comment later in this chapter. Let's continue to explore the name of God as it is written in the scriptures. We have learnt time and time again about the iniquity of the children of Israel, who were always running after other gods and ignoring their own powerful God. So as their lips became unclean, and unworthy, He began to put subtitles on His name, because unclean lips should never call upon His Holy Name. Read Isaiah 6:5-7: "Then said I, woe is me! for I am undone, because I am a man of UNCLEAN LIPS, and I dwell in the midst of a people of UNCLEAN LIPS; for mine eyes have seen the King, the Lord of Hosts.

Then flew one of the seraphims unto me, having a live coal in his hand, which he had taken with the tongs from off the altar:

And he laid it upon my mouth, and said, Lo, this hath touched thy lips; and thine iniquity is taken away, and thy sin purged." The scriptures do not lie, unclean lips must not call on the name of the true God.

We are still exploring God's name given unto His people, from time to time. Names like GOD OF HOSTS.
Amos 5:27: "Therefore will I cause you to go into captivity beyond Damascus saith the Lord whose name is the GOD OF HOSTS." He was also called JEHOVAH. Today's Christians still call Him by this name, but this name was also changed from the days of Isaiah, as you read in Isaiah 12:2 "Behold God is my

salvation; I will trust and not be afraid; for the Lord JEHOVAH is my strength and my song; he also is become my salvation."

Isaiah 26:4: "Trust ye the Lord forever. For in the Lord JEHOVAH is everlasting strength." If we look very carefully you will notice, that the name Jehovah was not known in the days of Moses. Another pinch of proof that God changed His name regularly. In the next scripture this is explained. Exodus 6:3 "And I appeared unto ABRAHAM, unto ISAAC, and unto JACOB by the name of God Almighty, but by the name JEHOVAH was I not known to them."

Psalms 68:4: "Sing unto God, sing praises to His name, Extol Him that rideth upon the heavens by his name JAH and rejoice before him." Note here that His name has been changed again to JAH. The name the Rastafarians use.

The name of God varies according to time and events. For the longest period He was called the God THAT LIVETH, then it had been changed again to the God THAT LIVETH IN TRUTH, but still this was not the ultimate. Before we get to today's name let's see the scriptures, as promised. Jeremiah 23:7: "Therefore behold the days come saith the Lord, that they shall no more say, The LORD LIVETH which brought up the children of Israel, out of the land of Egypt." This scripture confirms that God continued to change His name to His people for in the same book of Jeremiah 4:2, truth is added to the God that liveth. "And thou shalt swear, The LORD LIVETH IN TRUTH..." Anyhow the most used name for God and more relevant had always been THE GOD OF ABRAHAM, THE GOD OF ISAAC and THE GOD OF JACOB. A short cut to His identification would be THE GOD OF ISRAEL. As we read in Isaiah 43:3: "And I will give thee the treasures of darkness, and hidden riches of secret places, that thou mayest, know that I, the Lord which call thee by thy name am the GOD OF ISRAEL."

When you read what He said in Exodus 3:15: that His name would forever be, the God of ABRAHAM, the God of ISAAC and the God of JACOB, you will come to realize that all other names had been changed except this, for even Jesus called upon the Father, the Spirit ABBA in Mark 14:36: "And he said ABBA FATHER, all things are possible unto thee."

Let's see who the Father is to us. The Father is the Spirit, and Jesus kept reminding us who He is in Matthew 22:32: "I am the GOD OF ABRAHAM, the GOD OF ISAAC and the GOD OF JACOB." In Mark 12:26: "And as touching the dead that they rise, have ye not read in the book of Moses, how in the bush, God spake unto him, saying I am the GOD OF ABRAHAM, and the GOD OF ISAAC, and the GOD OF JACOB." Acts 3:13: "The GOD OF ABRAHAM, and OF ISAAC, and OF JACOB, the GOD OF OUR FATHERS, hath glorified his son Jesus."

There should be no confusion, among God's children, when it comes to His IDENTITY. Christians everywhere, black Christians in particular, shout the name Jesus all of the time, not knowing that it is not affective. Never call on the name Jesus alone. JESUS represents FLESH. When he was born of the woman MARY, his name was to be called JESUS by physical lips. Luke 1:31 "And behold, thou shalt conceive in thy womb, and bring forth a son and shalt call his name JESUS. In other words Jesus is just another Jewish name. There are a lot of Jesuses around even today, but only one CHRIST.

THE CHRIST represents the SPIRIT, or ABBA THE FATHER; Matthew 16:20 "Then charged he his disciples that they should tell no man that he was JESUS THE CHRIST." Acts 17:3 "Opening and alleging, that Christ must needs have suffered, and risen again from the dead; and that this JESUS, whom I preach unto you, is CHRIST."

If you believe that Christ is God, then you know what His name is, for the name of GOD ALMIGHTY is now known from the time He made contact with Moses in the burning bush, and throughout the lifetime of JESUS on earth. This name will remain until His second coming, when He will tell His people, the Israelites, His new name. Revelations 3:12: "Him that overcometh, will I make a pillar, in the temple of my God, and he shall go no more out. And I will write upon him the name of my God, and the name of the city of my God which is new Jerusalem, which cometh down out of heaven from my God, and I will write upon him my NEW NAME."

Now that we know what name to call upon let's find out how to call on the name of the God of Abraham, the God of Isaac, and the God of Jacob. **Praying with your hands clasped and your eyes closed while on your knees is wrong.**

This was the way the pagans prayed to their Sun god, and other false gods. Let's see what the scriptures say in Isaiah 44:17-18. "And the residue thereof he maketh a god even his graven image, he falleth down unto it and worshippeth it, and prayeth unto it, and saith, deliver me for thou art god. They have not know nor understand, for he hath SHUT their EYES, that they cannot see, and their hearts, that they cannot understand."

Isaiah is not mixing words here. He is talking in this entire chapter of the wrong ways people try to pray to any god they feel like. They couldn't understand. Like Jesus said in the New Testament that they will be calling on a lord, but He doesn't know them. It is very important to know whose name you call upon, and how you call upon it. Most Christians if not all of them, make it their duty to be calling on the name Jesus, not realizing that there is absolutely no spiritual affect in the name Jesus. Jesus is just another name that represents man. The CHRIST is the symbol of the resurrection, the CHRIST is the symbol of our Father. II Corinthians 11:4 "For if he that cometh preacheth another Jesus, whom we have not preached, or if ye receive another spirit, which ye have not accepted, ye might well bear with him." You may also read Matthew 7:21-23: "Not every one that saith unto me Lord, Lord, shall enter into the kingdom of heaven, but he that doeth the will of my Father, which is in heaven. Many will say to me in that day. Lord, Lord have we not prophesied in thy name? and in thy name have cast out devils? and in thy name done many wonderful works? and then will I profess unto them, I never knew you; depart from me, ye that work iniquity." which means calling on false gods without knowing. For they too are called gods and lords.

Let us get back to the subject of how to call upon Him. There are three ways to pray. One: lifting up hands and eyes toward heaven. Two: kneeling with your face to the ground, and three extending hands up towards heaven while kneeling. Daniel 12:7: "And I heard the man clothed in linen which was upon the waters of the river when he held up his right hand, and his left hand unto heaven, and swear by him that liveth forever." Psalm 63:4: "Thus will I bless thee, while I live, I will lift up my hands in thy name."

This was Solomon's favourite way of praying after his father David.

100

I Kings 8:54: "And it was so that when Solomon had made an end of praying all this prayer and supplication unto the Lord He arose from before the altar of the Lord from kneeling on his knees with his hands spread up to heaven."

It is hard for me to understand that all these instructions are written in the bible on how to pray yet Christians still find another way in direct disobedience to God. I Timothy 2:8: "I will therefore that men pray everywhere lifting up holy hands, without wrath and doubting."

Let's read again how the method of praying has not changed from the time of Moses, Abraham, Daniel, Samuel, David, Solomon and all of God's people to the time of Jesus. For this is how Jesus prayed. Matthew 26:39: "And he went a little further, and fell on his face and prayed saying, O my Father..."
Mark 14:35: "And he went forward a little, and fell on the ground and prayed." Now if Jesus prayed like this, what excuse do your Christian teachers give you for their way of praying?

We dealt with how our fathers before Jesus prayed. We have read how Jesus prayed. Now let us read in Revelation (meaning to come) which gives us instructions for today's society. Revelation 4:10: "The four and twenty elders fall down before him, that sat on the throne and worship him that liveth forever and ever, and cast their crowns before the throne..." Revelations 7:11. "And all the angels stood round about the throne, and about the elders and the four beasts, and fell before the throne ON THEIR FACES and worshipped God."

There is no other way to pray, that is written in the holy book of God. Again you have the choice of worshipping the pagan way, or the way taught us by our fathers before us.

To conclude this chapter will be to open the gates of communication between you and your God. Fall on your face and call upon HIS NAME, THE GOD OF ABRAHAM, THE GOD OF ISAAC, and THE GOD OF JACOB, THE GOD OF OUR FATHER ISRAEL, and you will hear Him, for He would have heard you. Do not be fooled anymore, our very survival as a people, depends on how we serve the God of our fathers. Christianity has done enough, to wreck us. We cannot allow it to destroy us. READ REVELATION 18:4. And may your eyes be opened.

HEAVEN BELONGS TO GOD

Let me tell you point blank, you cannot go to heaven in the skies, where you were told you will go when you die. The answer is **NO**. The elevator doesn't work. If you were planning on hitching a ride, the operators are on strike. If you have a lot of money, you can't even buy it, because it is not for sale.

Now let me tell you why. As a boy, I was told by my mother, who was the nicest person that I have ever known, that I should always be a good boy or I would never get to heaven. Bad boys go to hell. My mother meant that with all her heart, like a lot of other mothers, fathers, and teachers out there. This is another lie started by Christianity to subdue the subordinates, and to keep the oppressed, oppressed.

First they teach you that everything white was good, because God is white, and black people were born to be slaves, because God cursed them. Therefore they must learn to obey their masters or they will go straight to hell. If they obey, then they will go to heaven, and do you know what's funny? Everybody believed it, even today.

Some slave owners even believed it themselves because it was in the writings of Paul in the holy scriptures. I Timothy 6:1, Colossians 3:22 also in Titus 2:9-10. If you read all these scriptures by Paul, in the eyes of the slave master, Paul would be on his side. In teaching these scriptures it would be hard to convince otherwise, but Paul himself was in mental slavery.

He was a blackman born in Tarsus in Asia which was under Roman rule and Greek influence. He had no other choice, because most of his students were Gentiles, and heathens, pagans to the core. Paul tried to do a job of teaching spiritual things to physical people. He tried to tell them that they had a chance of being close to God, hoping that they would become knowledgeable and would practice the truth. That was never to be. They chopped his head off in 67 A.D. and distorted his writings with their own interpretation, and then gave you Christianity.

Jesus Himself never spoke of the world, in the context of all the world being saved. Jesus spoke of the world only to find His lost sheep, the children of Israel. But I am not here to condemn or to judge, only to set the record straight. Timothy gave his reason

slavery or master-servant relationship. In a
you can't win, don't fight. <u>I Timothy 6:5</u>.
ings of men of corrupt minds and destitute of the
that gain is godliness, from such withdraw

up. Wasn't God's people enslaved by the
were a mighty nation, and were subdued and
ey fought back? Did not God Himself make
? so the power of God, could have been stronger
he people take notice? Would it have been wise to
die? or wait to fight with God at your side and
answer these questions, you will see that Paul is

orting slavery, but is being wise as a serpent. It
tures that were mainly used since the publishing of
was right around the same time of the slave trade.
lave trade began in 1609, even though
istory books places it in the year 1619,
mes version of the bible was published in

eaven that is above the earth. There is heaven upon
ch is really the earth, and there is paradise, where
for the coming of the Messiah. Let's see what the
e to say about all this.

heaven which is above the earth, you, or no one else
can go. Jesus Himself said in <u>John 3:13</u>: "And no man hath
ascended up to heaven, but he that come down from heaven, even
the Son of man." Also in <u>John 7:34</u>: "Ye shall seek me, and shall
not find me, and where I am thither YE CANNOT COME." These
statements cannot be made stronger, since it is coming from the
authority. Yet we read in <u>Nehemiah 1:9</u>: "But if ye turn unto me,
and keep my commandments, and do them though there were of
you cast out unto the **utter most part of the heaven,** yet will
I gather them from thence, and will bring them unto the place, that
I have chosen to set my NAME there."

Here heaven is not above earth, but on the earth. God has
always intended to make the earth as heaven, if His people
behaved properly. It never happened, that's why sometimes He
referred to the earth as heaven, but not as a kingdom of heaven.

You will discover that the heaven spoken about by God through Nehemiah (referring to the laws of Moses) is indeed the nations on earth.

Nehemiah 1:8: "Remember I beseech thee, the word that thou commandedst thy servant Moses, saying, if ye transgress, **I will scatter you abroad among the nations**." then you may read verse 9. This should make it clear that you cannot go to heaven above the earth, where you were told by some Christian teachers and philosophers.

Let's look at it this way. We read that Jesus was the Son of David, but Jesus said, that He was from above. If Jesus then was from above, so would be His father David. Wouldn't that be fair to say? But David did not come from heaven, never went to heaven, and never saw heaven. Acts 2:34: "For David is not ascended into the heavens, but he saith himself, the Lord said unto my Lord, sit thou on my right hand."

This scripture proves that Jesus the Christ was only using David for his earthly kinship. How would David sit on His right hand, if he can't go to heaven where Christ is? The answer is in what Jesus told the malefactor on the cross next to Him. Luke 23:43: "And Jesus said unto him, verily I say unto thee, today shalt thou be with me in **PARADISE**."

You may now ask, where is paradise? Paradise is like Jerusalem, an earthy Jerusalem and a spiritual Jerusalem which is the New Jerusalem. Paradise is like flesh, that differs from flesh, one natural and the other spiritual. Paradise is like the Garden of Eden built with purity on earth, but now only mentioned parallel to perfection. To conclude. PARADISE is heavenly, but not in heaven, neither on earth, but like unto a spiritual Garden of Eden. Revelation 2:7: "He that hath an ear, let him hear what the spirit, saith unto the churches, to him that overcometh **will I give to eat of the tree of life, which is in the midst of the Paradise of God**."

We can now safely say that paradise and not heaven is where God's elect wait. If it were otherwise it would have been mentioned. Here is where Christianity has faltered, fooling and lying, getting people all worked up to go to heaven. They go out of their way to find scriptures to support their claim, and when they can't find any, they turn to their favourite word PHILOSOPHY, giving themselves the right to lie openly, while they utilize the meaning of another word, INTERPRETATION. I will continue to say, that this word is overused, or used by these so-called philosophical experts, providing them with excuses to reverse from direct confrontation with the truth. Just see if this statement is not familiar? "THAT'S YOUR INTERPRETATION OR, MANY PEOPLE INTERPRET THE BIBLE DIFFERENTLY." What stupid excuses, but Christians can always find a sympathetic ear. The bible is a plain and simple book, for those who are of the truth. Confusing to those who are of the lie, unrevealing to Gentiles, and downright mixed up for the hypocrites.

Let's return to the question of going to heaven, and to one of our very own, ABRAHAM. This is the scripture that your Christian teacher would read to you. Luke 16:19-31. "There was a certain rich man, which was clothed in purple and fine linen, and fared sumptuously every day. And there was a certain beggar named Lazarus, which was laid at his gate, full of sores. And desiring to be fed with the crumbs which fell from the rich man's table; moreover the dogs came and licked his sores.

And it came to pass, that the beggar died, and was carried by the angels into **Abraham's bosom**; the rich man also died, AND WAS BURIED.

And IN HELL he lift up his eyes, being in torments, and SEETH ABRAHAM AFAR OFF and Lazarus in his bosom.

And he cried and said, father Abraham, have mercy on me, and send Lazarus that he may dip the tip of his finger in WATER, and cool my tongue; for I am tormented in this flame.

And Abraham said, son, remember that thou in thy lifetime receivedst thy good things, and likewise Lazarus evil things; but now he is comforted and thou art tormented.

And beside all this, between us and and you there is a great gulf fixed; so that they which would pass from hence to you cannot; neither can they pass to us, that would come from thence.

And he said, I pray thee therefore, father, that thou wouldest send him to my father's house. For I have five brethren; that he may testify unto them, lest they also come into this place of torment. Abraham saith unto him, THEY HAVE MOSES AND THE PROPHETS, LET THEM HEAR THEM.

And he said nay, father Abraham, but if one went unto them from the DEAD they will repent. AND HE SAID UNTO HIM, IF THEY HEAR NOT MOSES AND THE PROPHETS, NEITHER WILL THEY BE PERSUADED, THOUGH ONE ROSE FROM THE DEAD."

There is no mention in what we have just read, that Abraham was in heaven, is in heaven, or the conversation was carried on between occupants of heaven and occupants of hell. As a matter of fact, hell was mentioned, after the rich man was buried, in verses 22 and 23, but nowhere was it stated that Abraham was in heaven, but I guess your Christian teachers would again use their most famous line. "That's your interpretation."

Again I say, when something is as plain as this, what interpretation would they be talking about? They also read John 14:2 "In my Father's house, are many mansions, if it were not so, I would have told you. I go to prepare a place for you."

Then they sing hymns about going to heaven, telling the poor parishioners that God has high rising apartment buildings with lots of vacancies up in heaven. This my dear reader is a lie. If you read verse 3 it will explain that this heaven that Jesus is talking about is going to be on earth, just like the original plan: "And if I go and prepare a place for you I will COME AGAIN, and receive you unto myself, that where I am, there ye may be also." Neither Jesus nor the prophets have ever said that you (man) were going to go to heaven, for if it were so, why then did Jesus teach His disciples to pray the first prayer of His coming? Matthew 6:10: "Thy kingdom COME, thy will be done on EARTH, as it is in HEAVEN." Luke 11:2: "And He said unto them, when ye pray, say, Our Father which art in heaven, hallowed be thy name. Thy kingdom come. Thy will be done, as in heaven, so in earth..."

Mark 9:1: "And he said unto them, verily I say unto you, that there be some of them, that stand here, which shall not taste of death, till they have seen the KINGDOM OF GOD COME WITH POWER."

So far we have read that this kingdom of God, (that is heaven) will be coming on earth, not the people from earth going to heaven, and you can't see that heaven until the coming of the Messiah. Revelations 22:12: "And behold I come quickly, and my reward is with me, to give every man according to his work shall be."

106

Daniel makes it very plain where the kingdom shall be. Daniel 7:26-27: "But the judgment shall sit, and they shall take away his dominion, to consume, and to destroy it unto the end. And the kingdom and dominion and the greatness of the **KINGDOM UNDER THE WHOLE HEAVEN** shall be given to the people of the saints, of the Most High, whose kingdom is an everlasting kingdom, and all dominions shall serve and obey him."

You can't go to heaven, and your Christian priests or whoever takes it upon themselves to teach from the book of the Israelites, that were not called to do so, are lyers. They all adopt the spirit of divination, which is not of the truth, for no such spirit can tell the truth. The spirit of divination speaks of god all the time but not the God written about in the Bible. You would know them when you see them, all you ever hear from their lips is god, god, god, jesus, jesus, jesus, and knows absolutely nothing about truth. Some collect money for spiritual services rendered, and claim to be doing it in the name of God. Some looking in dark places for spiritual supremacy. Acts 16: 16-17 "And it came to pass, as we went to prayer, a certain damsel possessed with a **spirit of divination met us, which brought her masters much gain by soothsaying:**

The same followed Paul and us, and cried, saying, these men are the servants of the most high God, which shew unto us the way of salvation". Do not be fooled with the words coming from such a person, because as you just read that even the so-called divine spirit was not of God. Deuteronomy 18: 10. "There shall not be found among you anyone that maketh his son or his daughter to pass through the fire, or that **useth divination,** or an observer of times, or an enchanter, or a witch"

Wait, wait I say on the Lord. It is easier to be in paradise, than to play God as Lucifer wanted to do, to go into the mountain of God and to ascend up to heaven.

When you read Nehemiah 1:9 you will see that it ended by describing this place which will be heaven on earth, where He will give them His name like in Revelations 3:12. The kingdom of heaven will be on earth. So I hope to see you all in paradise when I sleep in the everlasting rest..

107

CHRISTIANITY
THE LOST CAUSE

There's no Christmas - No Easter
No Christian lies - No fatman from the north
Bearing gifts in the night
No Jesus' birthday in the midst of the cold
This pagan custom was from days of old

No communion to take - No drinking of wine
Not at God's altar - All this is a lie
No wine must be drunk at the altar of God
Take wine for your sickness or visit the bar
Water is pure made by God
Wine is unholy - can be made by man

Muslims sold us - Christians bought us
Now all of a sudden they both love us
In these last days they wanna be our friend
We must ignore them - Let them go to hell
They have broken our bones and cut our flesh
And when we complained - They offered us death
Now both are saying to them we belong
But the bible is saying they both are wrong

Pope Julius said to Michelangelo
Paint all these heroes - Paint them as bright
They are so black - Paint them all white
The colour changed for Jesus and Mary
Their black skin exchanged for the white you now see

Who told you to pray the way that you do
Clasping your hands with your eyes closed too
The bible never said this is what you should do
With the man in Rome is how this began
Him playing a god controlling our land
Making new laws and forcing our hands
Baptising our babies - wetting their heads
All this pagan practise of worshipping the dead

Sabbath is gone now - Sunday stepped in
Another law made by Constantine
Christians are busy with so much to do
Changing God's laws for me and you

Christianity is lost - This evil must fall
Of all God's enemy
It's the worst one of them all
Read Revelation about the Great Whore
Then take that cross down from off of your door
If you look real close I know you'll find
This pagan custom that made us so blind
Is among the reasons that kept us in
This spiritual prison so we can't win

Our homes are jails, poverty and crime
The worst of it all is doing spiritual time
Let's return to our God - do it or bust
In this last 400 we have taken a lot
If Christianity lives then we have lost our guts
So let the Great Whore go - We have had enough
Don't drink of her wine
Just let her die

God's word must be a mystery, according to the scriptures written in <u>Colossians 1:26</u>: "Even the mystery which hath been hid from ages, and from generations, but now is made manifest to his saints." Because if it is not a mystery, then the Christian teachers are all liars, making a lot of Sunday noises about their own law, and are deadly silent about God's law. If this is not the foundation of the Christian church, then it must be sweaty and hot in winter time.

There is a lot not written in the bible that the Christian leaders teach. For instance, on the twenty-fifth of December (winter), shepherds were grazing flocks. This is the foundation of Christianity which presents you with a fat overindulgent man from the north, who plays God at this particular time of year, to lie to you and your children. This man knows when you are good and he knows when you are bad.

109

It is Christianity that tells you that a little white baby boy was born at this time and God sent this white baby, with his mother, during winter time, on a donkey, to black Egypt, to hide from white Romans. This is so ridiculous that I do not even want to comment further, for it is not only children who believe this lie, but adults too!

We must seek the truth in these vicious lies. First of all, do not allow anyone to tell you that there was no winter in Israel in those days, because there was, and it was cold, especially in the night. If it were not so, then the scriptures would not have stated in II Samuel 23:20: "And Benaiah the son of Jehoiada, the son of a valiant man of Kabzeel, who had done many acts, he slew two lion-like men of Moab; He went down also and slew a lion in the midst of a pit in **TIME OF SNOW**."

This scripture verifies that there was winter and snow. So how could these so-called shepherds be grazing their flocks at night time when it's much colder? This shows us how serious the weather could have been. Let's read Mark 13:17-18: "But woe to them that are with child, and to them that give suck in those days. And pray ye, that your flight, be not in the **winter**." Now if Jesus the Christ is warning you about the hazards of winter why would Mary take her baby and make her flight? Is this an uncompassionate God or what?

Let's look at another angle to those Christians who studied their biblical history in theological school. When did the Romans collect their taxes? Then I'll answer certainly not at winter time, or the twenty-fifth of December. Jesus was born when they were collecting taxes. Luke 2:4-7: "And Joseph also went up from Galilee, out of the city of Nazareth, into Judea, unto the city of David, which is called Bethlehem; (because he was of the house and lineage of David): **TO BE TAXED** with Mary his espoused wife, being great with child. And so it was, that while they were there, the days were accomplished that she should be delivered. And she **BROUGHT FORTH HER FIRST BORN SON**..." Therefore if it is a fact that they do not collect taxes during winter time, then it is also a fact that Jesus was not born on the 25th of December.

The 25th of December is a pagan holiday, which was celebrated long before the birth of Jesus the Christ. To honour the Sun god, Mithras the Roman name for the Persian god or Apollo,

110

or Raa, or Elagabaalus. All these various names mean one thing; paganism. The feast for the pagan gods begins on the 21st and the grand finale is on the 25th of December, and this is one of the corner stones of Christianity.

Let's now try as intelligent people of the Almighty to seek the truth. The truth is, seven is the number of perfection. We also know that God's domain which is the mountain of fire is in the seventh heaven. We know too that in Revelation John spoke of the seven churches in Asia Revelation 1:4: "John to the seven churches which are in Asia..." This scripture was given to John in the spirit in verse 10. We may also see the significance of the holy seven as in the number of spirits in Revelations 4:5: "And out of the throne proceeded lightings and thunderings and voices, and there were seven lamps of fire burning before the throne, which are **the seven spirits of God."**

We are trying to prove that if God had to come in the flesh that He would only come at a time of spiritual richness, and seven is the height of all spiritual realms. Jesus was born in the seventh month, the month of Tishri.

These are the twelve months used by the children of Israel:

1st - ABIB or Nisan March / April
2nd - IYAR or Zif.
3rd - SIVAN
4th - TAMMUZ
5th - AB or AV
6th - ELUL
7th - TISHRI, Tishrei, or Ethanim September / October
8th - HESHVAN, Cheshvan or Bul.
9th - KISLEV
10th - TEBETH or Tevet
11th - SHEBAT or Shevat
12th - ADAR February / March

This is what God said of the month of Abib in Exodus 12:2: "This month shall be unto you, the beginning of months. It shall be the first month of the year to you."

The scripture for the seventh month can be read in Leviticus 23:24-34: "Speak unto the children of Israel saying, in the seventh month, in the first day of the month, shall ye have a Sabbath, a memorial of blowing of trumpets, an Holy Convocation."

The fifteenth of the month reveals instructions from <u>verse 34</u>. This is proof that the seventh month is one of the holiest months of God. You afflict your souls and keep His sabbaths. By this you may already come to the conclusion on this topic. JESUS WAS BORN IN THE MONTH OF TISHRI - when they collected the taxes before the winter time. It is also the seventh month.

The mother of Christianity is the Catholic Church, who gave birth to her many children but steadfastly remained their mother. They have taken titles like FATHER, when the bible says in <u>Matthew 23:9</u>: "And **call no man your father upon the earth:** For one is your father which is in heaven." They use titles like Reverend, which is only reserved for God Himself. <u>Psalm 111:9</u>. "He sent redemption unto his people, he hath commanded His covenant forever. Holy and **REVEREND IS HIS NAME.**"

They have been pulling the wool over your eyes by giving you Isis and Horus, the Egyptian goddess, and calling them the Virgin Mary and Jesus. The bible never told you to worship His mother, as a matter of fact, Christ doesn't have a mother. Jesus called Mary His earthly mother, WOMAN and there is a scripture where He tells you that He doesn't have a mother. <u>Hebrew 7:3</u>: "Without FATHER, without MOTHER..."

Christianity has become the greatest con game of the centuries, by playing with people's emotions. Injecting everything of their philosophy that looks good and sounds good inside your mind. Unlike the doctor, who injects you with drugs to restore your physical health, Christianity injects the Blackman with lies for his spiritual death. Let's take one of the lies, that looks so good: **LOVE.** This is the most used, overused and misused word in Christianity. Christians use this word in every context even more than the people of God. Christianity tells you to love everybody; the bible never said that. Christianity tells you to pray for the world; God never said that and Jesus never did that. Now let me tell you how it all started.

First of all, the books in the bible which are mostly misquoted by Christians are the books of Paul, who was not a Jew. He was not even born in the land, making his story a perfect example of the separation of the Israelites. The Jews were the ones that remained in Israel. All the other eleven tribes were scattered according to the scriptures in <u>Jeremiah 18:17</u>.

112

"I will scatter them as with an east wind before the enemy. I will shew them the back and not the face in the day of their calamity." The majority went to Western Africa and they were called Jews and other names, until they weren't called at all. Some went close by, like Barnabas' parents who were in Cyprus where he was born, a Levite. Acts 4:36. Then there were some who looked on Rome as their mother country and went to Italy. Read Hebrews 13:24. This was the reason why Jesus said in Matthew 10:5-6: "These twelve Jesus sent forth and commanded them saying, go not into the way of the Gentiles, and into the city of the Samaritans enter ye not. But go rather to the lost sheep of the House of Israel." Matthew 15:24: "But he answered and said, I am not sent, but unto the lost sheep of the House of Israel." Jesus here wasn't saying what the Christians are saying. He is very blunt, undiplomatic and uncompromising. Paul was saying the same things, but in a diplomatic way.

In Romans 1:16: he says: "For I am not ashamed of the gospel of Christ for it is the power of God unto salvation to everyone that believeth, to the JEW FIRST and also the Greek." Here Paul is trying to say that as long as you worship the God of Israel, even if you are Greek or Roman, Gentile or stranger, you will be saved, but the JEW FIRST, and a Jew is an Israelite.

One of his most controversial statements is found in Galations 5:14: "For all the law is fulfilled in one word, even in this. Thou shalt love thy neighbour as thyself." Jesus also said that the two most important commandments are, First; have no other God. Second; love your neighbour as yourself.

Jesus was quoting Leviticus 19:17-18. "Thou shalt not hate thy brother in thine heart, thou shalt in any wise rebuke thy neighbour, and not suffer sin upon him. Thou shalt not avenge nor bare any grudge against **the children of thy people**, but thou shalt love thy neighbour as thyself, I am the Lord."

They are all the same statements, but Christians misinterpret Paul's statement claiming you don't have to keep the laws anymore, just LOVE. What Paul is saying here is, if you can't keep the law, you can't serve God. The love Paul wrote about is a brotherly love between Israelites. Galations 5:15: "But if ye bite and devour one another take heed that ye be not consumed one of another." Paul was speaking here to his people. He had a very difficult job to teach Israelites and to tell the Greeks and Romans

113

who he grew up with, that they too stood a chance. Even Jesus said that He prayed not for the world, but Christians do. Read John 17:9: "I pray for them, I pray not for the world, but for them which thou hast given me, for they are thine." Now let's define the word neighbour. Let's go to Zechariah 3:9-10. Here the neighbours of the Israelites were the ones who lived in the land, with whom they could sit down with under a fig tree and under the vine. In other words someone who worshipped their God and someone who they knew, but who was not born an Israelite. Christians want you to love the entire world, people you don't even know and the people that they do know are starving right here at home. What kind of love is this? Then again it's another trick by the Devil to deceive. If you don't give them your money they tell you that you're not of God.This is the same philosophy whose teachers segregated their own churches because of the Blackman. **IS THIS LOVE?** I guess the foundation of the North American Christian church may have a truthful answer, next time you see a member of the K.K.K. ask him. Let's go to another scripture in Matthew 15:26: "But he answered and said, it is not meet to take the children's bread and to cast it to the dogs." This is why they loved Paul, for he was giving the Gentiles hope, when Jesus wasn't. The acknowledgment of who God is, was, and will be is important. The laws, the statutes and the commandments are important. Denouncing all other gods and their customs is important. Knowing that the blood of the children of Israel runs through the Portuguese, Italians, French, Spanish, etc. makes it almost impossible to know who your brother is. As Paul said in Romans 9:6: "Not as though the word of God, hath taken none effect, for they are not all Israel, which are of Israel." Meaning the majority of Israelites today do not know about their religion and do not care. They would rather stay in the church where they can socialize, rather than turning to the true God.

This is a little history of this man-made religion. If you are a Christian then the Roman Catholic Church is the mother of your religion. You can stop talking to her, you can denounce her and some Christians openly abuse her, but it doesn't change a thing.

These are her two most powerful children: One born somewhere in the 16th century. Its physician was Martin Luther who was born November 10, 1483, who broke away from his spiritual father - the Pope and his mother - the Catholic Church.

114

The second physician was Henry VIII, who delivered the Anglican Church from its mother, because Pope Clement would not grant him a divorce so he could marry Anne Boleyn. There is not enough space for me to tell you about Calvin and a host of others. I can tell you though that your spiritual mother must be grateful to the pagan Constantine who in 322 A.D. gave you the Roman Catholic Church, that even today still worships the QUEEN OF HEAVEN.

Look how you have inherited some of her ways. You keep communion, drink wine, worship the dead (cross), believe in three gods (trinity), you pray to Baal (clasp your hands, close your eyes). Your slogans and your general way of worship is all spiritual inheritance of the worshipping of earth bound spirits and demons.

Augustine, whom you call a saint gave you Isis and Horus, the Egyptian goddess (Mary & Jesus). This black African who was born in 354 A.D. in Tagaste, a little town in Africa, went to Rome and adopted Christianity. All these are mere men that controlled the philosophy of the Christian church. How about allowing God to control the philosophy of your mind and love Him and not the Christian church. This is an example: the bible says in so many places that Saturday is the Holy Day that God has sanctified as His Sabbath. Constantine in 325 A.D. changed the Sabbath to Sunday, the day of the Sun god. Remember Lucifer loves too, for he loves his devils, his demons, for they obey him. Even though he is a liar, he still loves his own.

Let's take a close look at the parents of Christianity, the Catholic Church, the Pope and their customs. They worship the Queen of Heaven. The bible says it's not right. Jeremiah 44:17. "But we will certainly do whatsoever thing goeth forth out of our own mouth, to burn incense unto the **QUEEN OF HEAVEN** and to pour out drink offerings unto her. As we have done. We and our fathers, our kings, and our princes, in the cities of Judah, and in the streets of Jerusalem, for then had we plenty of victuals, and were well, and saw no evil."

To the Jews who had copied this pagan Egyptian way of worship there was no evil that they could have discerned. To them this seemed right. But to God it was a terrible thing to do, for the 23rd verse states: "Because ye have burned incense and because ye have sinned against the Lord, and have not obeyed the voice of

115

the Lord, nor walked in his law, nor in his statutes, nor in his testimonies, therefore this evil is happened unto you, as at this day." Today this is still the way of your Christian parents.

So strong and attractive are their ways of worshipping, that even in the days of old they managed to win over God's people, **the children of Israel.** Concerning early morning mass as they call it read: Ezekiel 8:14-16   MICAH 2:1   JEREMIAH 32:33-34 and especially JOB 31:26-28. All these scriptures will tell you about the abomination of rising up early, or turning your back on God's altar, or praying as the sun rises. It is all very sinful, but the priests have endorsed it to be o.k. and you have accepted and still practise it. It is a typical example of how this man made philosophy operates. God says in His book what is clean and unclean, and the swine being one that is unclean. Christianity says it is o.k. now to eat. The priests even pray over meals of pork and let you believe that they can bless the meal before you eat it. As I said before, the biggest time for all Christians is Christmas,   yet they openly omit Christ, that was not there in the first place anyhow, and made the signs official - **XMAS - without Christ.** Yet you shout with the breath that God had given you about His birthday. That is because Christianity again has played with your emotions, calling this time of year, "Peace and Love." So if you don't celebrate this pagan holiday, you are not of love and you have no peace within you. This is how they continue to trap minds with lies by putting you on a guilt trip. They tell you the Christmas tree came from Germany, but nobody took the time to tell you how it got to Germany, for the Christmas tree as they call it, was here long before Germany. Read Jeremiah 10:3-4: "For the customs of the people are vain, for one cutteth a tree out of the forest, the work of the hands of the workman with the axe. They deck it with silver and with gold, they fasten with nails, and with hammers, that it move not." The second verse of this same chapter tells you that this was the way of the heathen and people who are of GOD should not do these things. It's either the teachers of Christianity like the leaders of Rome, who are either playing gods, or they are all downright ignorant of the truth. Luke 6:46-47: "And why call ye me Lord, Lord, and do not the things which I say? Whosoever cometh to me, and heareth my sayings and doeth them, I will shew you to whom he is like."

To be a child of God is simple. Just understand what Jesus is saying in these verses for this is the true meaning of believing in the Lord Jesus, not just a spoken phrase, because you read it in the bible. "Believe in the Lord Jesus Christ and thou shalt be saved." It is empty without obedience to the words of TRUTH. That's why there is a choice that people of God would have to make. **God or Christianity, the truth or the lie**. For salvation is not in Christianity. John 4:22 states: **"Ye worship, ye know not what, we know what we worship, for salvation is of the Jews."**

When you understand what you read, only then will it make a difference. God's people, the Israelites need to be separated from a philosophy of doom, from man's imitation of God. Isaiah 24:4-6: "The earth mourneth and fadeth away, the world languisheth and fadeth away. The haughty people of the earth, do languish. The earth also is defiled under the inhabitants thereof; because they have transgressed the laws, thereof: because they have transgressed the laws, changed the ordinances, broken the everlasting covenant. Therefore hath the curse devoured the earth and they that dwell therein are desolate. Therefore the inhabitants of the earth are burned and FEW men left."

It is now up to you to be among the multitude or to stand with the few. If you don't believe me, believe the words of the Most High. Isaiah 44:21-22: "Remember thee O Jacob and Israel, for thou art my servant; I have formed thee, thou art my servant O Israel; Thou shalt not be forgotten of me. I have blotted out as a thick cloud thy transgressions, and as a cloud, thy sins. **RETURN UNTO ME,** for I have redeemed thee."

Let's take a look in the historical container and search through the rubble of slavery and its 400 years and what happened. For only with this knowledge we would be able to correct our mistakes, because this 400 years that we are in is very crucial.

Here is a brief 400 year history of each country that enslaved God's children and the sufferings of the children themselves for not turning to their God. For wherever they rule over their own people that country is in poverty and wherever they find themselves being ruled by others they are the ones in poverty.

According to history slavery was always there, including the enslavement of the children of Israel in Egypt, but lets talk about the last new world slave trade, after the Blackman lost power.

We will go back to the year 1440 when Antam Gonsalvez captured three Moors and gave them to Prince Henry the Navigator of Portugal as a gift. In 1442 these Moors handed over 10 other Africans to gain their freedom. Here is the beginning of the prophecy written about in the bible. This started in Portugal.

In 1492 after Columbus' discovery, the Spanish first enslaved the Indians who died because they were too weak and sickly. In 1505 the Spanish governor of Hispaniola (Haiti and the Dominican Republic) started importing slaves from Portugal. These first set of slaves had turned to Christianity from their own way of worship.

Later on, the Spanish conquered Cuba, Jamaica and Puerto Rico. In 1511-1518 slaves were shipped to these other countries. It was in 1518 that the Spanish, the Dutch and finally the British joined the Portuguese in buying slaves directly from the coast of Africa. In 1562 Sir John Hawkins sailed to Sierra Leone. He was the first to use force, and to instigate tribal warfare. He took three hundred African captives through the Middle Passage to the American colonies. Now let us go even further back to discover what history has taught us, but we weren't smart enough to learn.

ITALY (ROME)

For four years the battle raged on between the Romans and the Jews in Jerusalem that ended in 70 A.D. The Romans destroyed the temples of Jerusalem and made slaves of the Jews. The Romans were then militarily and economically powerful, winning all of the wars they fought until the Germanic tribes began to invade the western part of her Empire. This great nation came to an end when the northern Heruli tribe seized control from the Roman leaders and the Roman empire came tumbling down in 476 A.D. The end of the first 400 years after the birth and death of Jesus the Christ. After this fall Italy began its darkest days. It had no central government to keep order.

PORTUGAL

The Portuguese started the wheels of slavery turning in the mid 15th century. In 1775 a giant earthquake almost destroyed Lisbon. The next century was the British and French invasions.

The king fled to Brazil. The mid 19th century the end of Portugal's 400 years came to a close. It is now one of the poorest in Western Europe.

HAITI
Around 1505-1515 slaves were brought here. Then France took control of the western part of the Island in 1697. It was known then as Saint Dominique and the richest of the French colonies. The end of its 400 years was up in 1915. The United States sent in the Marines. Now Haiti is the poorest country in the western world.

CUBA
Around the same time as Haiti, slaves were brought here in the early 16th century. In 1762 the British drove the Spanish out. In 1763 the Spanish drove the British out and in 1895 Jose Marte fought Spain for independence. In 1901 Cuba obtained self government from Spain. Their 400 years came to a close in 1925 when the first dictator Gerardo Machado took power. Cuba drifted into poverty and now received huge subsidies from the U.S.S.R.

SPAIN
Spain went into the slave trade around 1498 to 1500. Spain was the wealthiest empire during her time of conquest. Spanish flags flew over California, Florida and the Philippines. She bounced back even after being defeated by the British in 1588 at sea and also in 1643 by the French on land. But she never came back after the end of her 400 years when she lost the Spanish American war in 1898. It was the end of her might.

BRAZIL
In 1538 Brazil began its importation of slavery from Africa. This country was so rich it sustained Portugal and at one point the ruler of Portugal sat on his throne in Brazil. Six hundred thousand immigrants came here between 1874-1889. The same amount of Israelites that left Egypt. The end of the 400 years for Brazil was

in the 1930s when the President was overthrown and Brazil got her first dictator Getulio Vargas. This was also the time of world depression and tension.

HOLLAND

Around the early part of the sixteenth century the Dutch joined the slave trade in Africa. In 1520 Protestants rebelled against the Roman Catholic Church. In 1579 the seven provinces were united under William I. In 1584 William I was assassinated. In 1609 they signed the Twelve Year Treaty. In 1684 the Republic of Netherlands was recognized by the treaty of West Phalia.

In this same century the Netherlands attained more wealth and power. Her flag flew over North America (New York) and a host of Caribbean and South American countries. After many wars with Britain and France she began to crumble. In 1830 Belgium became independent from the Netherlands.

Her 400 years came to an end in the 1920s and the 1930s when the Netherlands hit rock bottom and never regained her power. Hitler invaded in 1940.

JAMAICA

This island was discovered on Columbus' second trip in 1494. Around the early 16th century slaves were brought here. The Spanish ruled until 1655. Jamaicans rebelled in 1866. Slavery was abolished in 1830. After the rebellion in 1866 the British governor brought in Chinese and East Indians and introduced the banana as another major crop. In the early 1900s Jamaica slipped into poverty at the end of her 400 years.

We have proven all these facts in history so as to let you understand the most important 400 years is here. The period between 1609 when the slave trade started in the United States to 1611 when the holy bible was published. Only God knows what will happen then. It certainly won't only be a decline in economic growth for the United States, but we would watch North America slip into much more than a recession like the rest of the countries mentioned in this book. We will see total world confusion right before our very eyes. Then the true ISRAELITES will be known and few would be on the side of God doing battle at Armageddon.

Revelation tells you of frightening facts about Christianity and its leaders referred to as the **great whore**. The leaders of the world have drank her wine and fornicated with her. Please note that most western leaders are from Christian backgrounds.

Revelation 17:1-4: "And there came one of the seven angels, which had the seven vials and talked with me, saying unto me, come hither; I will shew unto thee the judgment of the great whore that sitteth upon many waters." (Many waters meaning many countries). Verse 15: "with whom the kings of the earth have committed fornication, **and the inhabitants of the earth, have been made drunk with the wine of her fornication.** So he carried me away in the spirit unto the wilderness, and I saw a woman sit upon a scarlet coloured beast, full of names of blasphemy, having seven heads and ten horns. And the woman was arrayed in purple and scarlet colour and decked with gold and precious stones and pearls, have a golden cup in her hand full of abominations and filthiness of her fornication." Read it again in Revelation 18:3-4. Do not even try to tell yourself that this is not the evil of Christianity that John is revealing to his people. For there is no other religion under the sun that is more powerful and rich than she is, that drinks the wine of fury. Remember too, the writers of the bible were not Christians but men of God, separating themselves from this evil.

There is a reason for all this confusion, and it is very clear to those who understand the bible. The bible is so simplified, yet so difficult for some to comprehend. This was meant to divide the clean from the unclean, the holy from the unholy, the chosen from the damned. This book contains black history, and yet at a time when the world seems to hate the Blackman, this black history book was cradled in the arms of the oppressor, claiming it to be his. Let's take a look at the history of this book THE HOLY BIBLE.

THE BIBLE

The original holy bible is a collection of books written in ancient times by the children of Israel. It is the most popular piece of literature ever written by any people.

The word "Bible" comes from the Greek word *biblia*, which means "books." It has been translated by many countries into various languages and published in more editions than any other written work.

In the old days of the Roman Empire, Latin was somewhat of an official language, and the word Testamentum was used for "Agreement." The English word is Testament.

So now we have the British, who took it from the Romans who took it from the Greeks, who stole it from the Egyptians that took it from the Israelites. **THE HOLY BIBLE** - the book of mystery.

TRANSMISSION

Transmission means to hand down, or the handing down of biblical materials. The children of Israel practised the laws and judgments as it was written on scrolls, and word of mouth, (in oral form). History began to emerge also on scrolls - collections grew and grew - eventually "books" came out. These were finally accepted as a guide line for the Israelites. The books were called *canon* (from a word meaning "rule"). The making of such list is known as canonization. This took place at various times for various books or collection of books during the time of the Israelites.

Transmission of the New Testament was easier, since men learnt by now how it was done, this was also in the time of the Romans, so there wasn't much interpreting to do. Most of the books were written in Greek and Aramaic. It was written in a somewhat different language, based on the same laws practised by the Israelites of the Old Testament. (It was the Old Testament that was studied by the apostles when they wrote the New Testament). The New Testament grew in popularity faster than the old, because in these books the teachers and rulers of Christianity could find more statements with double meaning befitting their belief. **There is nothing written about Christianity in these books.**

TRANSLATION

Old Testament - In its original form was written on scrolls in Hebrew. Later on with the disappearing of the original Hebrew language, other revised versions mixed with Aramaic were used, especially in Ezra and Daniel.

New Testament - These books were mostly written in Aramaic and Greek, because writers like Paul were educated in Roman, Greek and Aramaic, which is today called the Hebrew Language.

122

HOW IT ALL STARTED
As An Exported Commodity

Koine Greek (a Greek dialect) was used for the entire book. The bible began to change hands from the old Israelites then to the Egyptians, but its popularity grew among Gentiles and non-Israelites, the first being the Greeks. One such translation was called the **Septuagint** - meaning **"seventy"** actually it was seventy two Israelites, six from each tribe that wrote it for the PTOLEMIES of Egypt in the third century B.C.

The Samaritans also made a translation a century earlier of the first five books called the **Pentateuch**.

The Syrians (Syriac) made a translation of the Hebrew Bible called the **Peshitta**.

Scholars who claimed that they were Jewish made translations for popular use called the **Targumim** in Aramaic.

Latin translation (using the Greek Old Testament for that part of the bible) was called **Old Latin**, or **Itala**

Vulgate - a most famous early English translation made by Jerome (Christians called him a saint) in the early 4th century A.D. He used both the so-called Hebrew (Aramaic) and Greek versions for his translation.

The most famous edition of this version is the Sixtine edition, done at the order of Pope Sixtus V in 1590.

Old Israelites, known only as Jews then, helped Christians along with help from locals,translated the scriptures by hand into **Arabic, Gothic, Coptic, Ethiopic, Armenian,** and other languages. **German** - 1522-32 - Martin Luther. **English** - around the same time - William Tyndale - was quickly suppressed by the authorities.

English - 1535 - Myles Coverdale - published in Zurich. Many English versions followed. For instance: Matthew's Bible, Tavern's Bible, Geneva Bible, the Great Bible, and finally the Bishop's Bible - a revision of the Geneva Bible was published in England in 1568. **Rheims - Douai** - 1582 & 1610 English translation of the Vulgate. Eventually the word "Israelite" was no longer used on the lips of Christian teachers who replaced it with Christianity, even though Christianity was an insult to the people of God in those days, and is not found anywhere in the holy scriptures embracing the word of God.

King James Version - 1611 - basis of a revision of the Bishop's Bible. **(THE END OF AN ERA)**

Revisions of the King James - After the original King James bible continues a long list of revisions. The English Revised Edition 1881, the American Revised Edition 1901, Revised Standard Version between 1946-1952, The New King James, The Amplified bible etc. People have been often confused about the amount of time the BIBLE has been changed, and the variety of BIBLES available.

Let's take a close look and try to figure it out ourselves. Before now, **THE SAME BIBLE WAS TRANSCRIBED AND TRANSLATED INTO VARIOUS LANGUAGES. NOW THE SAME (ENGLISH) LANGUAGE HAS BEEN TRANSCRIBED AND TRANSLATED INTO VARIOUS BIBLES. WHY?**

The rulers of the society of the day took advantage of the spiritually weak. Now there is no more honesty of finding truth, but rape and exploitation of man's mind, especially the Blackman. So the searching for their rule of law continues as they print version after version, searching for themselves and finding nought. **And so on and more versions, and so on... etc...and more versions...**If you read carefully, you would have noticed the variety of hands, that the bible had passed through, and still remained black. It is amazing to note, the mystery of the power of God, for if it was possible, all these nations that suppressed God's children, and tried so hard to keep them in ignorance, were completely blinded of the real truth. Now we have a black history book distributed by white hands, and white skinned Edomites, revealing their black heritage, and proud of a history, that is uniquely BLACK.

In this 400 years that is about to close you will have to pick sides and make the most important decision of your entire life. Be on the side of God or go down with the great whore. For it is said in Matthew 24:14: "And the gospel of the kingdom shall be preached in all the world for a witness unto all nations and then shall the end come." The end of the last four hundred years will be around 2009-2011, or according to the official American history books, which states that slavery officially began in the year 1619 that will mean that the end of the 400 years will be **between the year 2009 and 2019.**

124

Christianity has been taught since Constantine and the pope of his day and all his henchmen who mixed God's truth with paganism and gave it to the world in the fourth century. The end never came. Therefore it must be a lie. Now the time is up and the time is now for God's truth. Come out of her my people. YOU MUST READ **REVELATION 18:4** AND TRY TO UNDERSTAND WHAT THE SCRIPTURES ARE TRYING TO SAY.

When you shall have read the above scripture, think about this. NO CHRISTIAN TEACHER THAT HAS STUDIED HIS PHILOSOPHY IN AN ADVANCED INSTITUTION SUCH AS A UNIVERSITY, COULD HAVE OBTAINED AN "A" IF HE FAILED IN THE STUDIES OF "PAUL". It is O.K. to fail on the studies of anyone else, excepting PAUL.

That is because all Christians were taught that Paul was a good Christian, and that he was a heathen before that. So Paul was made into a so-called CHRISTIAN ROLE MODEL, based on this vicious LIE. Here is a brief on my brother Paul, whom the Christians killed, and after his death, made him their god.

THE APOSTLE PAUL

WHO WAS HE

Romans 11:1 "I say then, Hath God cast away his people? God forbid. For **I ALSO AM AN ISRAELITE**, of the seed of Abraham, of the **tribe of Benjamin**."

II Corinthians 11:22-23 "Are they Hebrews? **SO AM I**. Are they **Israelites**? **SO AM I**. Are they the seed of Abraham? **SO AM I.** Are they ministers of Christ? (I speak as a fool) **I am more**;"

Philippians 3:5 "Circumcised the eighth day, **OF THE STOCK OF ISRAEL**, OF **THE TRIBE OF BENJAMIN**, an **Hebrew of the Hebrews**; as touching the law, a Pharisee; "

WHO WERE HIS BRETHREN

Romans 9:3-5 "For I could wish that myself were accursed from Christ for my **brethren**, my kinsmen according to the flesh: **WHO ARE ISRAELITES**; to whom pertaineth the adoption, and the glory, and the covenants, and the giving of the law, and the service of God, and the promises:

125

Whose are the fathers, **and of whom as concerning the flesh Christ came**, who is over all, God blessed for ever. Amen."

WHO DID HE PRAY FOR??

Romans 10:1 "Brethren, my heart's desire and prayer to God for **ISRAEL** is, that they might be saved."

Galations 6:16 "And as many as walk according to this rule, peace be on them, and mercy, and upon the **ISRAEL** of God."

THE HOUSE OF ISRAEL

Hebrews 8:7-10 "For if that first covenant had been faultless, then should no place have been sought for the second. For finding fault with them, he saith, Behold, the days come, saith the Lord, when I will make a new covenant with the **HOUSE OF ISRAEL** and with the house of Judah: Not according to the covenant that I made with their fathers in the day when I took them by the hand to lead them out of the land of Egypt; because they continued not in my covenant, and I regarded them not, saith the Lord. For this is the covenant that I will make with the **HOUSE OF ISRAEL** after those days, saith the Lord; I will put my laws into their mind, and write them in their hearts: and I will be to them a God, and they shall be to me a people:"

OTHER CONFIRMING SCRIPTURES

Romans 9:4, 6, 27, 31   10:21   11:7, 25, 26
I Corinthians. 10:18
II Corinthians. 3:7
Ephesians 2:12

THE CHILDREN OF SLAVERY SHOULD NO LONGER BE ENSLAVED IN STRANGE PHILOSOPHIES, CONFUSING INTERPRETATION OF THEIR BOOK "THE HOLY BIBLE", THE WORSHIPPING OF STRANGE gods WITH STRANGE PRACTICES, AND THEY SHOULD REJECT CHRISTIANITY IN ANY WAY SHAPE OR FORM. TEACH OTHERS RATHER THAN HATING THEM, FOR ONLY BY DOING SO, CAN YOUR LIGHT SHINE.

When I was blind
Lord I couldn't see
What Christianity
Was doing to me
They took away my God
And gave me
a false one
Changed His colour
Changed it all around
Even His hair
Gave me strange customs
And kept me in
FEAR

Oh what have I done?
I worshipped the dead
Clinging to a cross
They put it in my head
The history of my past
They ravaged and loot
Rearranged my head
And replaced the Truth
I went the wrong way
And the journey was long

Now the truth is in me
I know I was wrong
To worship Lucifer
Instead of my God
Now I know better
I'll shout with my might
Thank God Almighty
I'm an Israelite

ADVICE AND INSTRUCTIONS

WHAT'S IN A NAME?

Should you call yourself? Do you call yourself? Is it all right to give yourself a name or names? **What's in a name**? The underlined statement is always tossed around, but do we pay much attention to it? Most of us do not, but some of us take it very serious. During the Black Power craze of the sixties, when we had a clenched fist, and the Afro mop upon our heads, the urge and burning desire to identify ourselves with Africa was in the air and everywhere. Calling ourselves every name in the book, in total ignorance. Let us now try to examine all the facts.

I have come across names given to me by some people as theirs, who claim to be on the path of truth, names that they had given themselves. Names that are so far fetched and irrelevant, but they proudly carry them around explaining that "Since I became an Israelite I changed my name from the white man's slave-name." This statement might contain political substance on the surface, but it is not consistence with the word of God taken from our doctrine.

The Bible states, that in creation God named everything that was created by Him, then He gave that authority to man to call his seed by the name chosen by him. He gave Adam the power to name everything in the garden of Eden including Eve. He also told His children (the Israelites) how and when to name their offspring. In the beginning according to the scriptures (**Genesis 1:1-19**), everything was named by God Himself; the day, the night, the waters, the heavens, and the earth. Then God made Adam and gave him the authority to name the beasts, the herbs, and everything upon the earth. **Genesis 2:20**. Then God made woman, who was also named by man (Adam) as authority over her. **Genesis 2:23**.

Thus began the creation of names. The purpose for which names were created was for the identification of an individual or thing. It was given by the authority over that individual or thing, not so much as to be called by the individual in whom it was given, but by the authority who gave it. Even though the woman that God gave unto Adam, made with his ribs was an adult when Adam called her name "Eve" it must not be forgotten, that she was

128

then as a new born, while Adam was like the parent, for **he was the authority over her**.

Genesis 3:16. "Unto the woman he said, I will greatly multiply thy sorrow and thy conception; in sorrow thou shalt bring forth children; **and thy desire shall be to thy husband, and he shall rule over thee**." It should not be a statement for argument, because she had no name before "Eve." She was not born of a woman, she was the mother of all living. **Genesis 3:20**. This also is the beginning of man naming his seed; from Cain right through to the generation of Noah.

The first Chaldean to be called was Abram who was called a "Hebrew." This was the first man to be called by that name (**Genesis 14:13**) to separate him from the other Chaldeans, and to start the family of God. God changed his name to Abraham. **Genesis 17:5**. Sarai, his wife was also named by God in **Genesis 17:5** - she was called Sarah. Their first born son Isaac was also named by God in **Genesis 17:19**.

Lets pause here for a minute, something has been bothering me for a long time; coming from the mouth of a Muslim is understandable, for we know they are always looking for justification to their pagan philosophy, but for someone calling themself an Israelite it is deplorable and unacceptable to say that our father Abraham married his sister Sarah, which is a vicious lie, and quote **Gen.20:12**.How stupid can some people be, if God is our Father, are we not family? In that context isn't Sarah Abraham's sister? Let's take a look at the genetics of this matter. Who was Abram's father in the flesh? **Gen.11:26-29** "And Terah lived seventy years and begat **Abram, Nahor, and Haran**. Now these are the generations of Terah; Terah begat **Abram, Nahor and Haran.** And Haran died before his father Terah in the land of his nativity in Ur of the Chaldees. And Abram and Nahor took them wives; the name of Abram's wife was Sarai, and the name of Nahor's wife Milcah the daughter of Haran, the father of Milcah, and the father of Iscah" Please take note that it was Nahor who married his niece. This is how Abram's father Terah saw Sarai in **verse 31**: "And Terah took Abram his son, and Lot the son of Haran, his son's son; **and Sarai his daughter in law, his son Abram's wife**." Now you may read **Genesis 20:2-3** hoping this will close the mouth of all the lying tongues. Now let's return to the subject at hand, "Names."

129

We should sit back and take notice that when an adult name is being changed, God is the one doing the changing. Let me put it in a more simple form. Take circumcision as an example. When Abraham received the instructions from God to circumcise every male child on the eighth day; he, Abraham was ninety years old and Ishmael was thirteen. The command - **Genesis 17:11-14**. Instructions carried out - **Genesis 17:24-27**. We will notice that even though Abraham was circumcised at the age of ninety, it does not make it law for a man to be circumcised at ninety years of age. Anyhow, if you discover the doctrine of Israel, even if you are one hundred you must be circumcised. Even though on the discovery of the doctrine of Israel as an adult you must be circumcised, you may not however change your name.

OUR FATHER'S DUTY

To know the importance of names one must look carefully at God and His relationship with the Israelites (the children of Jacob), starting from Abraham to Isaac and how He named Jacob. **Genesis 32:27-29** "And he said unto him, What is thy name? And he said Jacob. And he said, Thy name shall be called no more Jacob, but Israel: for as a prince hast thou power with God and with men, and hast prevailed. And Jacob asked him, and said, Tell me I pray thee, thy name. And he said, Wherefore is it that thou dost ask after my name? And he blessed him there." **(Gen.35:10)**. The same was remembered by Elijah. **I Kings 18:30-31**. So it is written that it is the father or parent who must name the child, and not the child naming the parent or themselves. The clay has no power over the potter. **Roman 9:21**.

God was very plain with His instructions on how the children of Israel should call upon Him, and by what name. **Exodus 3:14-15** states "And God said unto Moses, I AM THAT I AM: and he said, Thus shalt thou say unto the children of Israel, I AM hath sent me unto you. And God said moreover unto Moses, Thus shalt thou say unto the children of Israel, **the Lord God of your fathers, the God of Abraham, the God of Isaac, and the God of Jacob, hath sent me unto you: this is my name for ever, and this is my memorial unto all generations**."

Let us also look at the story of Shadrach, Meshach and

130

Abednego. It is clearly stated in the holy scriptures that none of these names were given to them at birth by their parents, but by the Babylonian king Nebuchadnezzar in **Daniel 1:6-7**. In this situation they were called other names in the land of their captivity, but again, not by themselves, but by those who ruled over them. Like Shadrach, Meshach and Abednego, we were given names by our slave masters such as the ones we answer to. This is understandable, but then here we are, giving ourselves personal names; and as a people, calling ourselves Africans when God Himself has named us and called us the children of Israel **(Israelites)**. **Ezekiel 34:30**. He also said salvation is of the Jews (**John 4:22**), but here we are again looking for salvation in Christianity, calling ourselves Christians. Even Jesus identified Himself with one of His brethren in **John 1:47**. "Jesus saw Nathanael coming to him, and saith of him, **Behold an Israelite indeed, in whom is no guile**!" This confirms the fact that none of God's children in the bible were Christians, Muslims, or anything else but Israelites.

All those lacking in understanding of who they are, and have named themselves, it is important to go back to your original names given to you at birth by your parents, **"the authority."** To reject the authority of our parents is to reject the authority of God **"our Father."**

SURNAME AND ITS ORIGIN

If we notice carefully there are not any last names, or what we come to know as "surnames" today in the old testament; so where did it come from, and what is the purpose for last names? In biblical times one name was good enough, like Adam, Noah, or even Lucifer. The way it was done in the days of old; people identify themselves with their father. For instance: **Judges 5:12** "...Arise Barak and lead my captivity captive, **thou son of Abinoam**..." **I Kings 14:1** "At that time **Abijah, the son of Jeroboam** fell sick." **II Samuel 23:9** "And after him was **Eleazar, the son of Dodo the Ahohite**." If you look carefully you will see Eleazar not only being identified by whose son he was, but from which tribe or house his father was from.

God told us what name to call Him by, and He also gave our fathers names, that were first called surnames; not in the way we use it today. No last name was given by God to be used as a family name. God spoke to the individual. Not even the name of Israel was to be given as a family name. It was given to Jacob, while his offspring was identified with their father as, **"child of,"** or **"children of,"** or **"house of." There were no Rueben Israel, or Benjamin Israel.**

Even though the term family name, or last name started with Gentiles who tried to understand and copy our ways and failed, it still does not give us the right to change ours that was given to us by them. This action would put us in the same category with them at the same time playing God. The Gentile tried to identify his seed and lineage by adding son to his last name, for example, in Spain "ez," or in Denmark "sen." The Scots and Irish had placed the word "Gaelic" meaning son in front of the father's name, which created the word "Mac" the Gaelic name for son.

The English family name would be simply "Thomp**son**," or "Jack**son**," or "Robert**son**" etc. Please note how the European, that were known as Gentiles before, copied and changed last names even calling it surnames similar to our biblical fathers.

Surname, or a name other than the one given to you at birth was first used by God with Abram and Jacob, which were the most popular names that were changed. These were not added names, but the only name used, especially the one given Jacob in **Isaiah 45:4** "For Jacob my servant's sake, and Israel mine elect, I have even called thee by thy name: **I have surnamed thee**, though thou hast not known me." In the new testament it is no different. **Matthew 10:3** "Philip, and Bartholomew; Thomas, and **Matthew the publican**; **James the son of Alphaeus, and Labaeus, whose surname was Thaddaeus."** We can begin to see how it became common. Now most of us are carrying our father's last name, that came from our father's father, that came from his father, and so on. Today in some cases the mother's name is being used because of the ignorance of who the father might be, or a number of other reasons. But so far we have not seen once where a man of God (an Israelite) named himself in the holy scriptures.

To name oneself is to play a little god. The Khazarian who calls himself "Rabbi," or the man who teaches that in the Hebrew tongue God is called "Yahweh," then re-named himself by the same name "Yahweh" are perfect examples of blasphemy.

Children of slavery should never refer to themselves as

132

African, Muslim, nor Christian. They are children of the living God, Israelites, He is the God of our fathers, and also our God and our father - **the Authority**.

THE RIGHT WAY

We must look at the law laid down for Israelites and **this is the law**. At the birth of our children is when all the emphasis should be on **what** we should name our baby, **how** we should name our baby, and **when** we should name that baby, and certainly **none of this should take place in a place of worship,** but at the home of the child. On the eighth day the boys must be named by friends, relatives, and parents (brethren). On the fourteenth day the same for girls. This is the law written in **Leviticus 12:1-5**. The statutes or customs are found between the pages of the bible and in the historical events of our fathers in the days of old. The naming of the child and how it was done can be found in **Ruth 4:14-17**. "And the women said unto Naomi, Blessed be the Lord, which hath not left thee this day without a kinsman, that his name may be famous in Israel. And he shall be unto thee a restorer of thy life, and a nourisher of thine old age; for thy daughter in law, which loveth thee, which is better to thee than seven sons, hath born him. And Naomi took the child, and laid it in her bosom, and became nurse unto it. **And the women her neighbours gave it a name**, saying, There is a son born to Naomi; and they called his name Obed: he is the father of Jesse, the father of David."

The new testament also bears record of this custom. The story of John the Baptist, an Israelite whose father was a priest in Israel. **Luke 1:5**. Even before his birth John was named by God Himself, but it was on the eighth day that that name was given to him. **Luke 1:13**. First we must examine the whole truth about his birth and what took place on the eighth day. **Luke 1:57-60** "Now Elizabeth's full time came that she should be delivered; and she brought forth a son. And her neighbours and her cousins heard how the Lord had shewed great mercy upon her; and they rejoiced with her. **And it came to pass, that on the eighth day they came to circumcise the child; and *they* called him Zacharias, after the name of his father**. And his mother answered and said, Not so; but he shall be called John."

133

The only reason why the baby was not called Zacharias was because this baby was a special Israelite, but the custom of the people was still made very clear.

The story of the birth of Jesus the Christ, another Israelite is much the same. The instructions were given to the mother in **Luke 1:31**, while on the eighth day it was all done according to the custom of the people as they went to the house of Mary and Joseph. **Luke 2:21 "And when eight days were accomplished for the circumcising of the child, his name was called Jesus**, which was so named of the angel before he was conceived in the womb."

CONCLUSION

At birth is when your name is given to you, whether it is Babylonian, Egyptian or just a plain simple English, French, or Spanish name. That name at birth is registered and connected spiritually written in the book of judgment, and must not be changed for anything else.

This is a highly spiritual thing that should not be messed around or tampered with. Even though most of us were not given our correct names in the correct way, and at the correct time, we nevertheless answered to the name given us at birth and that makes that name ours. What is important now, is not to make the same mistake with our babies. Name them with the right names, and at the right time, and in the right way.

This statement is strictly for Israelites. I personally do not care about others and their pagan philosophies. I myself bear a Babylonian name, but I have answered to this name the same way Moses answered to his Egyptian one. **Exodus 2:10** "And the child grew, and she brought him unto Pharaoh's daughter, and he became her son. And she called his name Moses: and she said, Because I drew him out of the water." God spoke to him (Moses) in an Egyptian tongue calling him by the name he answered by, "MOSES" As it is written in the book of Isaiah, so shall it be." **Isaiah 66:22** "For as the new heaven and the new earth, which I will make, shall remain before me, saith the Lord, **so shall your seed and your name remain."** Changing our names is not going to make any difference, it's not yours anyway! and if we are not doing the things we are suppose to be doing, we will remain at the stage we're at right now following after the traditions of other men that are not of God. Let the heathen and the pagans worship their gods, but the children of Israel must obey their's. We must plan the future for our babies, teaching them from the womb, at birth, in marriage so that in their everlasting sleep they will be at rest, **God's Rest.**

OUR YOUNG MEN AND EARRINGS

This, what is called fashion today, is only another deplorable abomination in the face of our God. Earrings in the ear(s) of a Blackman (son of a slave) is a shame and disgrace. It clearly shows the ignorance in our mentality towards Egypt. God had cursed Egypt and the children of Ham, now all we ever hear about is Egypt. Our Fathers did the same thing and they suffered. **Numbers 14:27-45.** Now we are repeating the same mistakes. **Numbers 14:3-4** "And wherefore hath the Lord brought us into this land to fall by the sword, that our wives and our children should be a prey? Were it not better for us to **return to Egypt**? And they said one to another, let us make a captain and let us **return into Egypt.**"

The children of Israel wanted earrings like copy-cats of the Egyptians. He gave them, then took it back, again because of their stiffnecked ways. In **Isaiah 3:17-26. Ezekiel 16**.

We are indeed blind. Let us take a close look at this Egyptian symbol that our young men are so attracted to today.

We must first identify it with its owner, our enemy. In the book of Judges, you may read the entire story of Gideon, but in **Judges 8:24** Gideon is speaking to Israelites. "And Gideon said unto them, I would desire a request of you, that ye would give me the earrings of his prey **(for they had golden earrings because they were Ishmaelites)**.

The word prey here means of "lower calibre, victim, or enemy." I do not have to repeat myself to tell you about the Ishmeelites (Muslims). See **Genesis 21:9** for the connection of the Ishmeelites and the Egyptians starting with Hagar. **Verse 21** shows the continuation, and the part that Ishmael played as an Egyptian. Then read again about our enslavement by the Ishmaelites and Hagarenes in **Psalms 83:1-6**.

Now that we know to which people the earrings belong, let's

135

go a little further back and examine this spiritual but evil thing.

What piece of jewellry was identified with the making of false gods? Not rings, nor bracelets, nor footrings, nor any such, but Earrings. This Egyptian symbol that our black youths adore today bares an in-depth spiritual evil attached to it.

Exodus 32:2-4 "And Aaron said unto them **break off the golden earrings which are in the ears** of your wives, of your sons, and of your daughters and bring them unto me.

And all the people brake off the golden earrings which were in their ears and brought them unto Aaron.

And he received them at their hand, and fashioned it with a graving tool, after he had made it a molten calf: and they said These be thy gods O Israel, which brought thee up out of the land of Egypt."

When our father Jacob (Israel) spoke to God, God told him to put away the strange gods from among his people, and among the strange gods were earrings again.

Genesis 35 talks of the transformation of Jacob to Israel, a very important time in Israel's life, but God could not communicate with him because of the strange gods and the Earrings. In **Verse 4** his brethren handed over their Earrings. "And they gave unto Jacob all the strange gods which were in their hand, and all their **earrings which were in their ears,** and Jacob hid them under the oak which was by Shechem."

Common sense tells me that if God could not communicate properly with Jacob when his people had the Egyptian earrings in their ears; how is He going to communicate with us today with this very same Egyptian symbol?

Earrings in, or on the ears of a blackman is not only telling me he is an Egyptian, but is also the enemy of the God of Abraham the God of Isaac and the God of Jacob. It is also telling me that this man is still a slave for the enemies of God therefore cannot be of God, and is lost, and locked into physical, emotional, spiritual, and mental slavery as the scripture reveals the meaning of Earrings in the ear of an Israelite. **Exodus 21:5-6**. "And if the servant shall plainly say, I love my master, my wife, and my children; **I will not go out free.**

Then his master shall bring him unto the judges, he shall also bring him to the door or unto the door-post, and his master shall **bore his ear through with an aul; and he shall serve**

136

him forever."

An aul is a form of Earring worn by Israelite slaves. When you take a close look at all the ways where we've gone wrong, at all the wrong teachings we have been exposed to, yet we continue to cling to slavery.

No wonder we are in the shape we are in today. Crime and poverty, disrespect, despair and disillusion - hopelessness and fear. We cannot experience what happened in Egypt today, but we should try to understand why it happened, then we might be able to correct our mistakes. With all the gruesome memory of slavery, why would anyone in his right mind yearn to return to it.

SHOULD ISRAELITE MEN WORSHIP WITH THEIR HEADS COVERED?

Should men cover their heads in worship, or in public? Let us examine this question very carefully. Is this action in keeping with the laws of God, or the statutes of Israel? Are all Israelite men to wear bonnets or headdress? The Muslims, Khazarians, and Edomites do. The christian Pope does. Should we be copy-cats?

In **Exodus 28** we will find the instructions given to Moses, not for himself, a Levite, but for his brother Aaron. **Verses 39-41** states the pride that God had in the priests He chose for this particular office. You will also find this instruction in the next chapter (**Exodus 29**), particularly in **verse 9**. "And thou shalt gird them with girdles, Aaron and his sons, and **put the bonnets on them**: and the priests's office shall be theirs for a perpetual statute: and thou shalt **consecrate Aaron and his sons**." You will also find it in **Leviticus 8:13**. There is no evidence in the scriptures that the bonnet was worn any and everywhere in the streets by every Levite, or by every Israelite male. **Leviticus 10:1-11** clearly states that it was worn only in the inner court of the tabernacle of the congregation, and by chosen Levite priests. **Verse 1** states what the sons of Aaron did. They burned incense before the Lord when He commanded them not to. **Verse 2:** And there went out fire from the Lord and devoured them, and **they died before the Lord**." **No anointed priest should have burnt incense in the inner court before the Lord.** In **verse 3** it reads "Then Moses said unto Aaron, This is it that the Lord spake, saying, I will be

137

sanctified in them that come nigh me, and before all the people I will be glorified..." Nigh means "near." Everyone that comes near (inner court) will be sanctified and when you go to the people (outer court) I must be glorified. **Verse 4** states that Aaron other sons, who were also anointed priests could not even touch the dead bodies in the inner court. Aaron's uncle and his sons had to remove it. It also shows that it all happened in the inner camp (sanctuary), and had to be brought to the outer camp. **Verse 6** confirms, that it was the custom of the priests to uncover their heads in the outer court among the people, but on this particular occasion, because of the dead bodies, Moses instructed them not to. In this case, the covering of the head in public acts as a sign of mourning. **Verse 9** states that the priests shall drink no wine while in the tabernacle of the congregation.

MEN AND WOMEN

Jeremiah 14:1-4 "The word of the Lord that came unto Jeremiah concerning the dearth. Judah mourneth, and the gates thereof languish, they are black unto the ground; and the cry of Jerusalem is gone up. And their nobles have sent their little ones to the waters; they came to the pits and found no water; they returned with their vessels empty; **they were ashamed and confounded, and covered their heads**. Because the ground is chapt, for there was no rain in the earth, **the plowmen** were ashamed; **they covered their heads**." Note that the men covered their heads in shame and dishonour.

Covering one's head in Israel constantly, had always been a woman's dress code. Our grandmothers and their mothers always covered their heads. Let me try to prove to you that the covering of the head was for women generally in Israel starting from the books of the law. **Numbers 5:12-18**. In **verse 12** the scriptures stipulates "...**any man's wife**..." and **verse 18** reads "**And the priest shall set the woman before the Lord and uncover the woman's head**..." You can only uncover what was already covered. **Isaiah 47:1-2**.

AFTER AARON AND HIS SONS

In the days of the sons of Zadock, the same instructions were

138

given, and again only to the Levite priests of the inner court. First let me explain; the priests of the inner court were like Nazarites. They were anointed, and dressed spiritually, and not only with physical apparel, but with things that were uniquely spiritual. They were suppose to protect and keep all the precepts. They were different from a teaching or ministering priest The inner court as written in the books of the law, and the books of the prophets, even in the book of Revelation, was only used by such priests. Without this understanding we are only making fools of ourselves. These are the instructions given to those priests, in their time, in the book of **Ezekiel 44:17-21** "And it shall come to pass, that when they enter in at the gates of **the inner court**, they shall be clothed with linen garments; and no wool shall come upon them, whiles they minister in the gates of the **inner court, and within.** They shall have **linen bonnets upon their heads,** and shall have linen breeches upon their loins; They shall not gird themselves, with any thing that causeth sweat.

And when they go forth into the utter court, even into the utter court to the people they shall put off their garments wherein they ministered, and lay them in the holy chambers, and they shall put on other garments; and they shall not sanctify the people with their garments. Neither shall they shave their heads, nor suffer their locks to grow long, they shall only poll their heads. **Neither shall any priest drink wine, when they enter in the inner court.**" You may read **Leviticus 21:10-12**, or **Leviticus 9:23** for a confirmation of this statue. "And Moses and Aaron **went into the tabernacle of the congregation, and came out and blessed the people**, and the glory of the Lord appeared unto all the people." **Also Leviticus 16:23-24.**

I can close off this article now and not write another word. We should let the **Muslims, Khazarians and Edomites sweat this one out,** no Israelite should. The above is to prove to most of you who believe the lie that the New Testament is a Christian book and you are doing everything according to the old. Well you just found out how wrong you are. This is the very reason why I did not quote **I Corinthians 11:5-7** "But every woman that prayeth or prophesieth with her head uncovered dishonoureth her head: for that is even all one as if she were shaven. For if the woman be not covered, let her also be shorn: but if it be a shame

139

for a woman to be shorn or shaven, let her be covered. **For a man indeed ought not to cover his head,** forasmuch as he is the image and glory of God, but the woman is the glory of the man." **Verse 14-15** reads "Doth not even nature itself teach you, that, if a man have long hair, it is a shame unto him? But if a woman have long hair, it is a glory to her, for her hair is given **her for a covering**." You see now why I refused to quote the new testament. Do you also know that it is the custom of the Khazarian women to shave their heads? Just goes to show the ways of the Gentile Pagan are being copied all over again by Israelites. Oh what a mess. What a total shame.

We must try hard to understand this very important issue that make the liars look like fools. The inner court would one day be opened again to all who follow the doctrine of Israel, while the outer court would be for Christians, Muslims and Khazarians (Gentiles) and their philosophy. **Revelation 11:1-2.** "And there was given me a reed like unto a rod: and the Angel stood saying; Rise and measure the temple of God, and the altar, and them that worship therein. But the court which is without the temple leave out, and measure it not, for it is given unto the Gentiles; and the Holy city shall they tread under foot forty and two months".

This shows you clearly that **men who are indeed men do not cover their heads in a place of worship** unless they are not really men, but women that look like men. Men do not cover their heads, while wearing their garments of worship in the streets among people, impressing the ignorant; if you are not in mourning, or in shame, then you are not a man at all. Israelite men should never cover their heads in worship, this practice of a stupid looking skull-cap belongs to Gentile-pagans.The ancient looking black hat is a disgrace on the head of an Israelite..

Women cover their heads to worship. Get the picture?Men do not, and should stop wearing that stupid looking hat, trying to tell people you are religious. "Hats off to Israelite MEN"

Hear Oh Israel - the Lord our God - the Lord is One.

FOR MORE INFORMATION
ON
**THE BIBLE AND THE BLACKMAN
CONCERNING THE CHILDREN OF SLAVERY**

YOU MUST ALSO READ
THE FORGOTTEN ISRAELITES
God's Chosen People
&
THE WORD THE ISRAELITES AND THE DAMNED

<u>TO ORDER:-</u>

(1) THE TRUTH THE LIE AND THE BIBLE

(2) THE FORGOTTEN ISRAELITES

3) THE WORD THE ISRAELITES AND THE DAMNED

NAME_____

ADDRESS_____

_____

_____

PHONE (   )_____

Send me _____ (copies) of # 1
Send me _____ (copies) of # 2
Send me _____ (copies) of # 3

I enclose a $13.95 money order for each book.

Send all orders to:
FIFTH RIBB PUBLISHING
BOX 287 STATION E
TORONTO, ONTARIO
M6H 4E2 CANADA